SISTERS

SISTERS

by
Dr. Dale V. Atkins

ARBOR HOUSE
New York

Library of Congress Cataloging in Publication Data

Atkins, Dale V.
    Sisters.

    Bibliography: p.
    1. Brothers and sisters.   I. Title.
BF723.S43A85   1984   158'.24   84-12436
ISBN 0-87795-597-2

Manufactured in the United States of America

10 9 8 7 6 5 4 3 2

This book is printed on acid-free paper. The paper in this
books meets the guidelines for permanence and durability of the
Committee on Production Guidelines for Book Longevity of the
Council on Library Resources.

To Sylvia and Jerry
whose warmth
provided for Daryl and me
an environment in which we were loved
and encouraged to grow.
And to Daryl
with whom I continue to grow.

ACKNOWLEDGMENTS

This is, in many ways, a collaborative effort and would not have come to pass without the help, love, encouragement of many people in my life. So many people shared their stories with me not only at seminars, but also by inviting me into their homes to probe their innermost thoughts and feelings about their sisters relationships. Obviously, in order to protect confidentiality, I have changed the names of those interviewed.

Since I cannot acknowledge individually all of the friends, colleagues and family members, I wish to thank them collectively for their interest, ideas, trust, and caring. Specifically, there were people who encouraged me to pursue this endeavor in order that women could examine their own relationships in more depth. Nancy Brown Miller, Janet Weathers Etti Hadar, Gary Stolzoff, Norma Feshbach, Susan Lindner, Ruth Rabinovitch, Jane Schoenberg, and Bea Hart helped me define what it was I was after by asking the right questions and responding to me with love and understanding.

Richard Trubo is indeed a partner in this venture. His friendship, flexibility, support, and excellent editing skills were available to me whenever I needed them. I especially appreciate the faith in me that was demonstrated by both him and our dear agent, Mike Hamilburg. Mike's enthusiasm for the book was obvious from the moment he read it. His efforts linked me with Eleanor Johnson at Arbor House, whose encouragement helped me enormously.

To my friends at Rancho La Puerta I offer a special thank you for providing me with a healthful environment in which to create and review.

Finally, I want to thank my family for their love and support throughout the research and writing of this book. My parents, Sylvia and Jerry Atkins, have encouraged me throughout my entire life to pursue whatever goals I choose. They raised us in an environment filled with love so that my sister and I would grow with a respect for one another. They treated us as individuals. My sister, Daryl Roth, was the first and constant inspiration for this book. She continues to be one of the most important influences in my life and her comments and suggestions are present throughout. I love and value her and her treasured family.

CONTENTS

Chapter 1   Sisters—the Extraordinary Bond   13

Chapter 2   What Makes the Sisters Relationship
             So Difficult?   26

Chapter 3   How Families Limit the Intimacy of
             the Sibling Bond   50

Chapter 4   Communication—How It Helps and
             How It Hurts   63

Chapter 5   Why Parents Perpetuate Old Patterns   76

Chapter 6   Sisters, Husbands, and Lovers   93

Chapter 7   Assessing Your Relationship with
             Your Sister   109

Chapter 8   Starting Down the Path Toward Bet-
             ter Communication   116

Chapter 9   Sisters by Choice   138

Chapter 10   How Parents Can Encourage Their
             Daughters to Feel Close   153

             Bibliography   171

SISTERS

CHAPTER 1

SISTERS—THE EXTRAORDINARY BOND

"It's something deep that I have felt for my sister over these past seventy years. We have been through hard times and easy times and we're always there for each other. Perhaps I've learned more about the constancy of a relationship throughout life from her than from anyone else."

During my childhood, my older sister, Daryl, and I shared the back seat of our parents' white Chevrolet on weekend family outings—but an imaginary line divided the seat into separate, hostile camps. If Daryl's arm or leg strayed onto my turf, or vice versa, the car was immediately transformed into a battle zone, with bickering and shouting that even a game of States or Capitals couldn't silence.

But as clearly as I can recall these skirmishes, I can also remember quite different experiences with Daryl during these outings. Late at night, coming home from holiday dinners at our aunt's home just hours after one of our quarrels, my eyelids would become heavy and I'd snuggle next to Daryl and rest my head on her lap. The imaginary dividing line forgotten, she would gently stroke my hair and twirl my pony tail, and often I would feel so close to her that I'd try to fight off sleep to savor the moment. My big sister was taking care of me. These are among my warmest memories of childhood.

Today, three decades later, many of these elements endure in my relationship with Daryl. She is my dear friend, my ally, and although we now live a continent apart, I still look to her for support. Our personal life choices have led us down significantly different paths, but I know that Daryl will always be there when I need her, and I trust that she feels the same about me. Of course, all is not perfect— even though the back-seat battles are in the past, our relationship is still tested occasionally by a disagreement or crisis. But we have been strengthened—as individuals and as sisters—by what we have learned from our childhood experiences.

From the earliest years of life, the sisters union is one of the most emotionally charged of all relationships. My interest in the many facets of the sisterly bond has led me into several years of research, which has involved many day-long seminars on the subject conducted in all parts of the United States and Canada. I have consistently found that all women seem to want to talk about their relationship with their sister—regardless of whether they view it as a good relationship. Many women attend these conferences with their sister to affirm the positive relationship they have with one another, and to spend the day together; others come in search of explanations and answers for the problems that have led to estrangement.

In the seminars women first hear lectures that expose them to general research and theories about sisters and families. Then they listen and direct questions to a panel of four to five pairs of sisters recounting *their* life experiences. After recognizing the unique characteristics of their own sisters bond, participants are then able to share some of their feelings with their own siblings in small group settings led by counselors. Often, the seminars serve as a form of mediation between sisters.

The topics raised at these conferences include patterns of communication, old roles, issues of autonomy and independence, illness, loss of a sibling, the problem of dealing with aging parents, and spousal/partner choices. As the day progresses, it becomes clear that nearly all women seem to recognize the extraordinary potential for emotional fulfillment within the sisters bond—despite the difficulties that inevitably occur. Most of the women yearn for information and guidance on how to improve that relationship.

Listen to what women say: "My sister is not anything like me." "She's so much like me that it scares me; I see things in her I can't stand about myself." "No one has as much power over me as my sister; why can she make me so upset?" "My sister and I are in our fifties; so when we go back to our parents' house, why do we fall into the roles we played as teenagers?"

Many of us have learned more about life from our sisters than from anyone else. As we grow up, sisters can serve as teachers, models, problem solvers, confidantes, catalysts, challengers, socializers, protectors, and caregivers.

With a sister, you learn to love and to argue, to share and to spar. You can learn about closeness, friendship, and making compromises. As you watch your older sister develop breasts and begin menstruation, you start forming your own sexual identity. And when your teenage sister starts dating, you begin discovering and understanding the opposite sex. Our personalities and our lifelong behaviors are influenced significantly by our sisters, and our relationship with them serves as a training ground for all of our other relationships.

No wonder we feel so close to this other woman in our lives. No one knows better than a sister how we grew up, and who our friends, teachers, and favorite toys were. No one knows better than she the inner workings of our family, our parents' private and public selves. Although as an adult you and your sister may live in very different worlds, and may adapt to those worlds in very different ways, you are sharing a strong bond: the source from which you've learned about life.

Many women idealize the sisters relationship. In a recent seminar one woman said to her sister, "You know me better than anybody, and that's why I want you to understand and accept me. Why can't you value me as I am, instead of always wanting me to be like you?" We look to our sisters for unconditional love and support and are often shocked and disappointed when we don't get it. Millions of women go through their lives wishing, "If only I could talk to her," or "If only she was not . . ."

I am going to help you take a more pragmatic look at *your* sisters bond. I will help you set realistic goals and expectations for the relationship, thereby improving communication. This will enhance your understanding of the dynamics of your relationship with your sister, why it is the way it is, and whether it necessarily has to remain that way. Using the results of my own research, as well as an analysis and interpretation of the various comments of sisters on many issues, I will also explore the questions I am most frequently asked about sisters:

What is it that has bonded sisters so deeply?
Why can a woman often get along better with a friend, but feel a more intense tie with her sister?
How are friendships affected by a woman's relationship with her sister?
How has a woman's identity been affected by her sister?
How can women get along better with their sisters?
How can old familial roles be altered?
What happens when one sister is more successful than the other?

No matter how estranged sisters may feel from one another, few siblings ever completely separate. Often, the ties between sisters run much deeper than those between husbands and wives. True, some sisters may not have spoken for years, long after they have both forgotten the cause of their rift. Yet even the most alienated sisters feel ambivalent about the separation, conflicted by such issues as loyalty, envy or competition and convinced that, however traumatic the breakup, they should still be faithful and supportive. This is especially true in families who place a premium on loyalty and nurturing. Indeed, the ties are not easily severed. And no matter how distant you may feel from your sibling, when you see her living her life, even from a distance, you will probably wonder, "What would I do in her situation? How would I feel?"

Not long ago, I met with two sisters, Joanne and Darlene, both in their late twenties, who felt quite close to and protective of one another. However, they had a third sister, Susan, who had caused a disruption in their relationship. Susan was twenty-two, slender, attractive, and more career oriented than either Joanne or Darlene, both of whom were married, quite overweight—like their parents—and worked at jobs they didn't particularly enjoy. In appearance and lifestyle, Susan defined herself within the family by the fact that she was different, and, as a result of these divergent life choices, there was a long-standing estrangement between the younger woman and her sisters.

Were they not siblings, the older sisters might have been quite comfortable just dismissing Susan from their lives. "But I feel guilty," Joanne said. "Susan's my sister, and I feel that we should be close. I have such wonderful feelings for Darlene, and that makes me feel terrible about my estrangement from Susan. But although I want Susan back in my life, I resent some of her behavior. Whenever we're together, she puts demands on me, and wants me to take care of her. But I can't; I'm tired. I have my own child to care for. Still, I can't let go of Susan completely. She is my sister."

As relationships evolve, two sisters may become closer to one another than to a third sibling. In this instance, Darlene discovered she had even stronger feelings of loss associated with Susan than did Joanne, primarily because she and Susan had once shared a bedroom and had been quite close at the time. Darlene decided that she needed to reestablish her relationship with Susan—on her own terms, apart from Joanne.

You meet your sister in early childhood, and with life spans now often extending to seventy, eighty, or more years, you will know your sister for a greater length of time than your spouse or even your parents. It is not surprising, then, that most women I've talked to desperately want to maintain or reestablish a good relationship with their sisters. But most consistent and compelling is the desire for *acceptance* from one's sibling.

Unfortunately, that acceptance is too often lacking. But when it exists, the chances for a strong, rich relationship are dramatically improved. Consider Margo and Maureen. Opposites, they are quite comfortable with allowing the other to be different. As they were growing up, their primary sisterly models were their mother and their aunt, who were, Margo recalls, "like clones of each other. It seemed boring . . . they did everything together. Maureen and I vowed not to be like that. We wanted to be close, but still separate."

Today, at age thirty-two, Margo is an insurance agent, and Maureen, at twenty-six, is training to be a stockbroker after having worked as a blackjack dealer in Las Vegas. They disagree on many issues, from boyfriends to careers. But, says Margo, "Even though we disagree, there's never any judgment. We may not like what the other has chosen to do with her life, but we support each other in whatever decision is made."

Margo's and Maureen's ability to accept each other's life choices is due in part to their childhood environment. "Our parents never pitted us against one another," said Margo, "and we never had to compete. We never had to vie for our parents' love and attention, either. We somehow knew there'd be enough to go around."

But life decisions complicate many sisters relationships. When my own sister and I shared a bedroom as we were growing up, we often whispered late at night to one another from our respective beds, sharing secrets and fantasies about our lives and futures. These experiences are common, and if, as adults, one sister chooses a man (or a career, or a place to live) that the other had never anticipated, some women perceive this as a rejection of their shared fantasies and shared goals—a rejection, in effect, of them. If, for example, one sister moves far away from the family turf when she reaches adulthood, and the other stays in the general vicinity, the sibling who remains behind may very well perceive her sister's move as a rejection, an abandonment—especially if she is forced to assume added responsibilities in the process.

THE VARIABLES AFFECTING SISTERS

Not all sisters are as fortunate as Margo and Maureen. Dozens of variables can influence the sibling relationship, many dating back to the early years of childhood. From parental expectations to values, from family communication to stresses, they can all become obstacles to the formation and maintenance of a healthy sisters relationship.

Consider familial roles and labels, for instance, many of which are assigned by parents very early on to their offspring. These roles are tenacious, and often, once a sister adopts one, it can literally accompany her throughout life, affecting her personality, her behavior, and her relationships.

Listen to Regina: "My mother once said, 'Your sister is so sentimental and sensitive; it's lucky you're so strong, dear.' She honestly did not understand that she needed one strong child because my father had died, and so I basically became the strong one. It did have a lot of advantages, but it also left some scars that I'm still showing today."

Labels, too, can last well into adulthood. "The one that's still operative at age fifty-eight," says Regina, "is when a male friend of ours said to me, when my sister and I were twenty and twenty-two, 'I've always thought of your sister as a hothouse orchid, and you as a sturdy cactus.' Who wants to be a sturdy cactus?"

In a study by sociologists J. Bossard and E. S. Boll, eight roles that children often assume appeared again and again:

- *the responsible one.* Typically the oldest daughter, she assumes a parental role in the lives of her younger siblings. She is looked up to and provides direction to the other children in the family.
- *the studious one.* She is recognized by other family members for her "brains" and consistently does well in school.
- *the popular, well-liked one.* She has personal charm that wins her recognition within the family.
- *the socially ambitious one.* She is a "social butterfly."
- *the self-centered, isolated one.* She often withdraws from the family and, in adulthood, demonstrates a unique capacity for organizing her life when out on her own.
- *the physically weak one.* She is *perceived* as being ill more often than other family members.
- *the irresponsible one.* She withdraws from family responsibilities, forcing others to compensate.
- *the "spoiled" one.* Typically the last-born child, her needs and desires are routinely met by others in the family.

Sound familiar? You can probably identify with one or more of the above types. And if you're like many women, these roles may be ones from which you've consistently—

and unsuccessfully—tried to escape over the years. But family pressures (real or imagined) have kept them in place. Older sisters may want to get off their preachy pedestals of responsibility, whereas younger sisters may be just as eager not to be identified any longer as the "weird" or irresponsible one. For all, it's a tough job.

Listen to this forty-one-year-old mother of five who is both a counselor and the owner of a successful catering business: "No matter what I've done, I've always been considered a misfit. My mother is never going to approve of me. And that will be hard for me to accept until the day I die."

Another woman complained that she wishes she no longer had to be so "responsible" and could just "go crazy" for a couple of days. But, she added, turning her fantasy of escaping her role into reality "is out of the question"; too many people rely upon her as their citadel of conservatism and dependability.

Take Carol and Annie. Thirteen years apart, they have only recently shed roles developed over a lifetime. When Annie was born, the youngest of seven children, Carol took over the maternal responsibilities because their mother was ill. She continued to play that role throughout her younger sister's childhood.

When Annie was twenty-five, her husband was killed in an automobile accident, and she went to live with Carol. As in the past, Annie allowed her older sibling to take care of her, at least during her grieving period. During this time, the two women got to know each other and gradually began relating to one another as equals. Today, Annie and Carol still live together and have established a mutually respectful and empathic relationship.

Sometimes a crisis focuses attention on these labels,

forcing the individuals to examine and relinquish them. When a parent dies, for example, the older, "responsible" sister may feel too emotionally distraught to handle funeral arrangements, and for the first time, a younger sibling may take over the role as the reliable, dependable one.

At the age of thirty-nine, Jennifer detected a lump on her right breast. The diagnosis was breast cancer, a mastectomy was performed, and the long, slow recovery process began.

Jennifer, who had always been the strong and independent daughter in the family, had confidence that, with her doctor's help, she would fully recover. But Linda, her thirty-two-year-old sister—who had lived for years with an image of a sixties "flake"—was not so sure. In fact, she had convinced herself that Jennifer was dying and, consequently, was motivated and able to break out of her old role. "I was born on Jennifer's birthday. We look alike, we sound alike, people even mix us up sometimes, although we're very different individuals. She got breast cancer, and I'm really scared. It's very nerve-racking to think that may happen to me, too.

"It did feel good, though, that I could be there for her, not to have her lean on me, but just because we could be so close." For the first time, *Linda* became a caretaker of her older sister, assuming a new function within the family.

Interestingly, Jennifer was not conscious of the role reversal that had occurred until Linda had pointed it out to her. "I think that the experience of losing a part of my body and almost dying made me realize how much my sister means to me," Jennifer said. "She has really been a 'rock,' and I've been able to depend on her. And that's okay for me to do, because I don't allow myself to depend on too many people."

Jennifer has recovered, and with Linda having broken free of her traditional familial role, the relationship between the sisters has changed dramatically. Today, for the first time in their lives, they are relating as equals.

Parental influence on the sisters relationship persists well into adulthood and very often the motivations for that involvement are not entirely selfless. When, for example, a mother tries to include herself in her daughters' relationship, the motive is often to validate or strengthen her own position within the family. She may compare one sister to another, not always realizing the effect it may be having on each of her children—as individuals and as siblings.

Take Rebecca and Julie, who are both artists and in their forties. When Julie was about to enter her first art show, her mother visited, eyed the works of art, and promptly announced, "Well, they're nice, but Rebecca paints with *real* oils." To this day, Julie doesn't know the difference between her oils and Rebecca's *real* oils, and she wonders, "Why couldn't Mom just let us both be artists in our own right?"

Sometimes mothers use one sister to run interference for them: "What's your sister doing?" "You should tell your sister that . . ." This manipulative kind of behavior can inhibit a positive relationship between siblings.

Parental favoritism can also have a devastating impact upon a sibling bond. Each time Tommy Smothers complained, "Mom always liked you best," millions of TV viewers must have nodded their heads, identifying immediately with the sentiment. Most mothers (and fathers) would deny showing any favoritism for one child over another, but whether in fact this is the case is almost irrelevant. If one woman *perceives* that her sister really was loved more, even if this is not so, it can significantly affect the way the sisters get along throughout their lives.

No matter how profound the problem in your present sisters relationship, improving that bond *is* possible. If you examine your own personal situation—your family, your present life, your values and beliefs—you can create a prescription for developing communication and interaction between you and your sibling. Step by step, I will show you how to enhance this vital sibling bond.

CHAPTER 2

WHAT MAKES THE SISTERS RELATIONSHIP SO DIFFICULT?

"I wonder if I'm trying to make my sister more like I'd like her to be and less of who she actually is."

If you had any idea how many divergent elements influence you, your sister, your parents, your home life, your dreams, and your expectations, you wouldn't even have to ask the question that serves as this chapter's title—it would be obvious! But it's difficult to sift through the myriad variables affecting your life without feeling overwhelmed. The first step is to recognize the factors—most of which you as children had no control over.

A SEPARATE IDENTITY

From the earliest days of childhood, and continuing throughout adult life, the sisters relationship can be characterized by conflict. Even the closest sisterly bonds seem to have their share of stresses and strains. A major cause of this phenomenon is each woman's personal quest for a separate identity within the context of the family unit. Women have reported more difficulty asserting their individuality and separating themselves from their sisters than from any other family members.

This may be particularly difficult for twins and triplets. A thirty-five-year-old identical twin who is a psychiatrist told me, "I feel as if we have had to be alike and different at the same time. That has been the theme of our lives. We have tried to be different, but being different is not something we were supposed to be because then we would get into competitive issues, and that was difficult for the people around us as well as for ourselves. . . . I feel we were programmed to be the same and to be different."

Her twin sister, an architect, remembered that their grandmother was never able to tell them apart: "She didn't just confuse names, she really couldn't tell us apart. People don't think it matters so they don't try to distinguish between you. Well, it does matter. It was really startling when I asked our mother about this, and she admitted that at times she couldn't tell us apart either. She continued to dress us alike until the seventh grade. What was the hardest, though, was asking my mother what I was like as a little girl, and she didn't remember whether something happened to me or to my twin."

Other twins have related similar experiences. Sadie and Pauline, seventy years old, were always referred to as Sadie-Pauli, or Pauli-Sadie. They hated the assumption behind this, but they had great difficulty separating from each other because their family relied upon connecting them. Parents can encourage twins to stay together, to

become each other's "best friends," thus becoming emotionally entwined. When Pauline got married at age sixteen, Sadie had difficulty coping with the loss. The very
next year she, too, married, but the relationship was not a
happy one. Even so, she remained in that marriage for
twenty-five years, feeling unable to face the world alone
after being "deserted" by her twin.

Danielle and Denice, another set of twins, twenty years
old, were both students and roommates at a California
university. When Danielle decided to take a summer vacation in Europe alone, Denice felt she was being deserted
and decided to hasten a pending marriage. Danielle returned from her travels to find her sister married. Now,
with one married and the mother of a new baby, and the
other still a college coed, the foundation of their relationship—their lifelong reliance on and commitment to one
another—has been transformed.

Sisters who are not twins, of course, may experience
similar difficulties. A sister's motivation for asserting her
individuality may vary. Some women have told me that
identifying with their sister might have threatened their
position in the family. Anna, for instance, believed it
would have been "catastrophic" to identify with her sister,
Jane, because during their childhood the one with the
power in the family was her brother and she had assumed
that identifying with him would be her ticket to recognition within the family. She also shied away from her sister
because, as with many younger sisters, Jane's activities
and attitudes frequently angered her parents.

But the strain between the sisters was not irreparable.
Today Anna and Jane live in the same city and see each
other frequently. Each woman eventually needed to know
that the other was willing to relate in a candid, straightfor-

ward manner. When they reunited, Jane finally admitted to Anna that she was extremely happy living a quiet life with her gay lover and their respective children.

Jane, a divorcée, has six children of her own, and Anna now spends a lot of time with all of them. She shares all of the holidays with Jane's family, has Sunday brunch with them, and considers her sister her closest friend.

"It's amazing that my parents always made me feel as if Jane was bad," Anna said. "Until I was living on my own, I never felt she was someone I could get to know and like. Now I can't imagine my life without her and her children. The sexual preference thing is so insignificant in our relationship; that's part of who she is, and she is the most wonderful, caring, sensitive woman I have ever met! Fortunately for me, I have her as a sister! It's my parents who are losing out on knowing her."

Family dynamics, then, can seriously (but not necessarily permanently) impair the sisters bond. Consider the case of sixty-year-old Robbi. Raised in a traditional Italian-American household in Brooklyn, with two older sisters who were attractive and popular, Robbi was considered the tomboyish and studious one. Her father even told her that she had been his last chance to have a son, and as a result she was extremely sensitive to his disappointment. Exacerbating her insecurity was the fact that her parents repeatedly told her that she was not a "good catch." When she left home after high school—after the family's college tuition money had all been spent on her older sisters—she married and had just one daughter, reasoning that an only child would not encounter the unhappy family interactions she'd confronted as a child.

The strain of those early experiences resulted in limited contact between Robbi, her sisters, and her mother for four decades. Finally, when Robbi was in her late fifties, she was contacted by one of her sisters, who expressed a desire to bridge the gap between the two of them. They met and made a commitment to communicate regularly. Today they are concentrating only on each other as their relationship heals, for they believe that to involve their mother or other sister could disrupt their recuperation process.

During childhood, girls often experience extreme un-easiness when they feel excluded from a family "clique." To compensate for this rejection, they may make special efforts to attach themselves to a variety of girls in school, and they may begin to store up feelings of resentment toward the sisters who excluded them. Recently four sis-ters, ranging in age from thirty-seven to fifty-five, at-tended a sisters seminar together. The two eldest siblings were identical twins, and the other two were seven and fifteen years younger respectively. The "middle" sibling, Ellen, convinced that the twins and her younger sister had formed their own "clique," spent her childhood feeling like the odd one out. As an adult, she tried to dispel this feeling by inviting Louise, the twin with whom she thought she would have the best chance of developing a good rapport, out to lunch. "She's the one sister who called me after my divorce to see how I was doing. I really felt she sincerely wanted to know if I was okay. I was tired of being left out of things and wanted to establish some kind of a relationship with at least one of them."

But Ellen was upset when she learned that Louise had told the other two sisters about their impending luncheon: "Why did she have to do that? I just wanted to meet with her privately. At this time, I feel safer with her than the others. As a child, I felt as if there was a conspiracy and I was always being discussed without my knowledge. Now, they're talking about me again."

Let's take a step back to look at this situation from both sides. Perhaps the other sisters, upon hearing about Louise's invitation, had only talked about how surprised and pleased they were with Ellen's desire to communicate with one of them; they may have heartily welcomed the gesture, hoping that the time would soon come when all of them would receive such a call. However, from Ellen's perspective, building a relationship with one sister was all she could handle at this time, and she was distressed that once again she was being "discussed." To her, that came as a sign that the clique was still impenetrable, and she broke the date. But all was *not* lost. Louise and Ellen *did* discuss the problem, and Louise assured her that from then on everything between them would be confidential. Also, although they agreed that all the sisters might do things together in the future, for now the interactions would be strictly one-to-one.

Sometimes, the clique is not between sisters, but between parents and their offspring. Joanne, for instance, is six years younger than her sister, Dorothy, and though they have a good relationship they wanted to be even closer. Joanne, now thirty-five, commented on the many changes they had been through in their lives. Like Ellen, she felt there had once been a closed club in the family, consisting in their case of her sister and their parents: "I felt the only way to gain entrance into the group was to be the clown. As a result nobody ever took me seriously, and it was very tough sometimes; now, at the ripe old age of thirty-five, they still don't take me seriously! And all because I felt I needed an entrance card into the club."

FAMILY SIZE

Family size can also significantly affect the quality of the sisters bond. In large families, where very often religion, family, and peer influences pressured the mother into bearing lots of children, sisters may relate differently to one another than if their mother had really wanted all of them. Why? Families with "unwanted" children often experience the stresses and strains of parental ambivalence, causing difficulties not only between generations but also between siblings.

Large families can present other problems, as happened in one family of eleven children, where the sisters referred to themselves as a whole team, with their father as a "coach." The eldest child, Rose, thought her mother expected her to be the model for all the younger offspring: "She made me feel that they were little puppets who would do whatever I did. When it came to the little kids, they were told to look up to us older kids, especially me because I was always made an example of. But I never really got a chance to relate to them as my sisters and brothers. For a long time I wanted my parents to apologize to me for making me the perfect example, for putting so much pressure on me, and for putting a barrier between me and the other kids. But I used up so much energy being angry that I just decided to let it go and not blame them. They really didn't know what they were doing. I had to forgive them."

Children from large families have usually learned to share, wait their turn, and appreciate each other as members in the group that is pitted against the adults. (As one sister in that family of eleven put it, "We were the USA.

Our parents were the USSR.") Children in large families are also often encouraged to be like one another as much as possible, thereby leaving little room for rebelliousness and individuality. On the positive side, when these children enter school, the fact that they have had more experience relating to other children near their own age makes it easier for them to function well within a peer group.

BIRTH ORDER

In families of all sizes, birth order can influence sibling interactions. Bossard and Boll found that the oldest child tends to assume responsibility for the other siblings—especially when the oldest child is a girl, in which case she gradually takes on the role of the second mother. Elizabeth Forer and Helene Arnstein contend that the firstborn child is task oriented and throughout childhood is the object of high expectations from the parents.

Birth order may also have an impact not only on the future relationship between the sisters, but on their work and marital ambitions as well. As the eldest child in a family of ten, a California politician felt as if she had already raised her kids and was therefore not interested in having any more. She had learned how to parent, she said, because her mother was so busy with the very young ones that the responsibility for the older ones fell on her shoulders. She attributes much of her present leadership skills and capabilities to her role within the family.

Hennings and Jardin found that of a hundred Fortune 500 female business executives, 75 percent were firstborn girls and the others were single children. A Rhode Island psychologist, who studied career choices of people from various positions within the family structure, found that most of the lawyers he interviewed were firstborn children. Perhaps early development of their decision-making capabilities and their tendency to take responsibility seriously influenced their attitudes toward achievement and ambition as adults.

Some investigators have examined how birth order may affect the physical and psychological development of children. In Dr. Helen Koch's classic study of siblings in two-child families, a large sampling of six-year-olds from two-parent households was matched in terms of socioeconomic status, residence, and age in an effort to assess the effects of ordinal position, sex, and spacing of children upon personality development. Koch found that firstborn children tended to have a stronger conscience, were more responsible, less aggressive, and more intellectually curious than second-born children. However, the effect of ordinal position was dependent on the sex of the siblings and the age spacing between them. Same-sex siblings who are close in age intensified their influence on each other during childhood.

Research demonstrates that parental behavior is different toward each child in a family, but it is not clear whether or not this is solely a result of a child's position in the family constellation. In examining parental behavior toward first, middle-born, and youngest children, it has been found that the parents' expectations are not the same for each child—demands are greatest on the firstborn and the least on the youngest child. Parental expectations also may have a lasting impact on the child's personality.

Brian Sutton-Smith and Benjamin Rosenberg agree that the special parental attention traditionally given to the firstborn child—more exclusive time with the parents, as well as a greater opportunity for identification with them—affects the child well into adulthood.

Helene Arnstein viewed the position of oldest child as a potential source of problems. To help the firstborn adjust to the presence of a younger sibling, Arnstein advised parents to make special efforts to meet the older child's emotional needs. When the child has difficulty adjusting to the loss of primacy, empathy rather than annoyance was advised. If the firstborn child feels there is enough love to go around, then the younger child gradually becomes less of a threat, and there is greater likelihood of a more harmonious sibling relationship throughout life.

The firstborn can maintain a special relationship with the parents even after her younger siblings come on the scene. In a study of female role modeling, Brian Sutton-Smith and Benjamin Rosenberg found that, of eighty female children and adolescents who were equally distributed into four ordinal positions, firstborns were found to be most strongly identified with their parents, compared to children in other ordinal positions. Other research shows that firstborn children also feel pride in their role as the older, more experienced teacher of their younger siblings. Since they have received undivided parental attention in their early years, firstborns tend to be giving and responsible. But as suggested earlier, many firstborns also complain about the burden of responsibilities that are sometimes thrust upon them before they are mature enough to deal with them. Having to bear heavy responsibilities at an early age may cause firstborn children to become overly conscientious and develop a possibly somber disposition.

Helene Arnstein cautioned that being given too much responsibility may increase the oldest siblings' resentment of their younger sisters and brothers. But in my own study of older sisters' perceptions of responsibility in families with and without younger hearing-impaired siblings, I found that it was the *perception* of the amount of responsibility—not the actual amount or type of responsibility—that was the crucial factor in determining the older sisters' attitudes toward their roles in the family.

A common complaint of many older sisters as adults is that they do *not* want to continue as the responsible ones or the role models in the family. They want to feel freer to be "crazy." But one sister complained that she didn't feel as if she could be "crazy" because if she did "lose it," who would be there to take care of things?

Many older sisters will actually *ask* their younger sisters to stop perceiving them as role models. A fifty-seven-year-old attorney kindly requested that her younger sister allow her to step down from her pedestal because "it's getting too wobbly up here!" When such a request meets with a positive response, this seems to contribute significantly to helping sisters develop a more adult, egalitarian association.

Now let's turn to the younger sibling for a moment. Researchers themselves disagree over whether the most apt description of the youngest child is "outgoing" or "spoiled." Ask some sisters, though, and they will most likely say spoiled. There may be more to this than you think. After all, don't most youngest children receive a lot of attention from their older siblings? But don't they also have to follow in their older siblings' footsteps (at school, in the community, etc.)?

Later-born children are often exposed to fewer anxieties because they come into a world where there is less parental anxiety about child rearing. An exception is in the case of families where the firstborn child is disabled or chronically ill—the parents are likely to feel overwhelmed and tend to treat the second, "nondisabled" child as a "first" child.

Research has shown that the effects of birth order extend into many areas of adult life. Toman suggests that when choosing a marital partner, people should pay attention not only to *their* position in the family, but that of their potential spouse. Why? Because specific needs and behaviors are more easily accommodated if those needs are already familiar. For example, a good match could be an older sister and a younger brother, since the older sister is accustomed to looking after others, and the younger brother is used to being looked after.

CULTURAL EXPECTATIONS

In many cultures, societal expectations demand that sibling responsibilities and interdependence last a lifetime. These responsibilities include domestic tasks, cooperative child rearing, defense, rites-of-passage ceremonies, arranging of marriages, and providing of marriage payments.

Consider the case of Halla and Rah, two sisters from Saudi Arabia. Recently they both attended a program for the rehabilitation and education of Halla's hearing-impaired son because they knew that soon Halla would have to return to Saudi Arabia for a few months to fulfill obligations with her husband, at which point Rah would take over the parenting role of the boy.

This kind of behavior is intrinsic to many Eastern cul-

tures. During the major immigrant waves at the turn of
the century, men would travel to the United States and
Canada and then, instead of sending for their wives first,
would send for the eldest son and/or daughter so that
their spouses could remain in the mother country and look
after the children there, while the older sister assumed
responsibilities for the new arrivals in the United States. In
many cultures, sisters are actually the prime caregivers.
These and other tasks may determine the child's role
within the family. Sisters from various cultures who attend
my seminars are used to perpetuating an interdependent
relationship with their siblings—particularly younger
ones—regardless of whether this is acceptable to others in
the family.

As Thomas Weisner has observed, expectations for
one's children may be either accepted or rejected by each
youngster. When three generations of a particular family
attended a sisters seminar in Los Angeles, it became clear
that the two sisters from the oldest generation had specific
expectations for their "girls"—expectations that were not
universally accepted by the younger siblings. Because of
strong pressure for everybody to "pitch in," the children
were accustomed to a high degree of interdependence.
These older sisters could not understand their grand-
daughters, who were totally independent of and rivalrous
with each other and tended to ignore familial responsibilities.

AGE SPACING

Sibling relationships can also be influenced by age spacing in the family. Helen Koch found that a two- to four-

year age difference between siblings was most threatening to the older child. By contrast, if the firstborn was three years old when the new baby arrived, she was apt to become anxious over the possible loss of her ability to nurture. If the firstborn was only a year old when the new baby arrived, her self-image was still so diffuse and ambiguous that she probably would not regard the baby as a major threat or competitor for parental attention. If the older child was five or older when the new sibling arrived, she was much more independent of her parents and was less threatened by a newcomer in the family.

Koch's observations were corroborated by Lamb in a study of interactions between preschool children and their infant brothers or sisters. When siblings were the same sex and separated by less than two years there were differences between them. In pointing out that today's parents are having fewer children and those children are spaced about two years apart, Stephen Bank and Michael Kahn contend: "This narrow age spacing can force children into contact, dependence and competition and heightens opportunities for mutual influence" (*The Sibling Bond*, Stephen P. Bank and Michael D. Kahn). Years ago families were generally larger, age range between children was greater, and older siblings were often out of the house by the time the younger ones were in grammar school. Much older sisters, as adults, experience the age gap narrowing if and only if they make an effort to interact with one another on a fairly regular basis.

Invariably, a number of sister pairs attending the seminars are separated by tremendous age differences. Recently there were three sets of sisters with thirteen, sixteen, and twenty years, respectively, between them. As adults, they had become reacquainted because of a desire to get to know their siblings as they are, not as they had idealized them. Helgola Ross and Joel Milgram found that sibling closeness (and thus the ability to bridge age gaps) may evolve through the sharing of experiences, individual and family values, and physical space.

One participant summed up the issue of closeness this way: "Nobody but your sister knows what your Aunt Ruth is really like. No one else knows that when Aunt Ruth comes to visit, your mom takes out her painting and hangs it up, and when she leaves, mom puts it back in the closet. Nobody but your sister knows what your history is really like."

This is especially true for women close in age. For those separated by a large age gap, they may have to make an effort to get to know each other well and to become closer, because in many cases they neither shared a room nor values. If they were from different generations, their perspectives may have reflected their respective times.

Often a life crisis can bring together sisters who have been separated—psychologically and logistically—for many years; for example, when one sister loses a child or a spouse. But other factors can also be the catalyst for the healing of alienated relationships. Some sisters simply decide that it is time to get to know each other better, and that it will not happen without each person investing emotional energy. In adolescence, because sisters often have their own very personal set of values and morals, they do not feel comfortable telling their older sisters much about their lives; but as they mature, these young women often take the initiative to reapproach their sister, newly aware that each has something of value to share with the other.

SEX EXPECTATIONS

Remember Robbi, the woman mentioned earlier in this chapter whose father had hoped she would be a boy? As that story emphasized, our sex significantly affects the way each of us relates to and is treated by not only our parents, but our siblings as well. And Robbi's story is not an unusual one.

Consider Eva and Sallie, two sisters in their mid-forties, the eldest of eight children raised in Louisiana. Eva, the firstborn, was treated as if she had been a son. Her father trained her to be a carpenter, plumber, and all-around handyperson: "I didn't have time to look after the babies because I was always working with Daddy and the boys, learning a trade."

Sallie, on the other hand, was primed to be the surrogate mother. To this day, she resents her sister for "not doing what she was supposed to do, as the first girl, and forcing me into the role of mother when I really wanted to go out and play with the boys and learn a trade, too." Sallie never married or had children, and she still regrets it; but she did participate in raising Eva's three children, as well as her other nieces and nephews.

Eva has told Sallie that she does not feel she is the one responsible for their life situation, and she resents being blamed for it. After several recent discussions, Eva offered to help Sallie go back to school and learn a trade (she always wanted to be a carpenter), and suggested that the two of them open up a "Sisters Carpentry" business in their hometown. It was their first step toward freeing themselves of old patterns.

ECONOMIC FACTORS

A family's economic status can have an effect on the relationship of sisters from childhood well into adulthood. In many cases, parental income is not enough for each sibling to have what she wants, and a rivalry ensues over whose desires will be met most often. In instances when a disability or illness strikes, aside from the stress accompanying this event, there are usually tremendous financial restraints upon the family; several siblings of handicapped children have told me (with considerable guilt) of their disappointment at being denied something because their disabled brother or sister was in need. Whenever parents are under such financial strain, choices are often made in favor of the most needy; although, intellectually, children can accept this, they may emotionally feel cheated. Interestingly, in families where children contribute part of their after-school earnings to the family budget, there is less of a feeling of favoritism and more of a feeling of collective support.

THE PARENTAL FACTOR

From many women I hear, "How can we be from the same parents? We are so different." To this I respond, "Were they really the same parents?"

Nobody remains the same with the passage of time. People and marriages go through transitions. Parents may become separated or divorced, or their relationship may substantially improve. When the parents do divorce, they may become more preoccupied with the demise of their marriage and the shock of being single again than with child-centered issues. Or, by the second or third child, a mother may want to begin or resume a career, or return to school, and may feel conflicted about choosing a life that excludes her children. Ultimately, grandparents or child-care workers may take over more of the parenting. Or the mother, tired of carpooling to dancing school, gymnastics, scouts, and soccer practice, may decide that she would like to begin a social life with new friends. Or she may start using alcohol or drugs. In the process, younger children may have to deal with a mother or father who is absent or inattentive, relying instead upon older siblings for the support and continuity once provided by their parents.

Lisa, a seventeen-year-old, recently spoke of her twenty-two-year-old sister, Diane, as her "new mother." Her actual mother, newly divorced, was exploring the single life as well as her new professional life as a high-ranking, frequently traveling executive. Lisa, in turn, assumed an older sister/mother role with her fourteen-year-old sister. Both she and Diane took turns going to the fourteen-year-old's piano lessons, doing homework with her, and taking her shopping. Lisa described the family situation this way: "I just couldn't count on my parents anymore. They had their lives to live, and although I understood it, I didn't like it. Sometimes I felt as if I wasn't that important anymore. I used to feel that all of us kids were number one. Lately, I haven't felt that. But we are all number one to each other, and right now that's what counts. I know I can rely on my sisters no matter what. I guess I'm growing up faster than I intended."

Another woman, Juliette, misses her sister terribly and recalls with tears the only close times they spent together.

"When we were young, my father married this other woman. Maria and I had each other, though, so we were really close. That's why it's so hard now to be apart from her, geographically and emotionally."

Maria lives in Massachusetts, married to a man with whom Juliette does not get along. For years Juliette has been asking her sister to visit her in California without her husband, and finally, at this writing, Maria has decided to make the trip. Juliette is scared. "Over the years, to maintain some relationship with Maria, I didn't tell her certain important facts about my life and lifestyle that I thought she'd disapprove of. Now, I have to face her and be honest about all of the lies I told her over the years. But I don't want to perpetuate the lies anymore."

How desperately Juliette and other sisters want to hold on to even the most tenuous sibling relationship! They will even concoct stories to create the illusion of closeness. For Juliette, this was better than not having any relationship at all. Until our discussions began to make her feel more secure with herself, she had been uncertain about risking the truth.

Juliette is not alone in making difficult but emotionally rewarding moves to renew sisterly ties. Coreen and Lillian were separated from each other for more than fifteen years. Since their parents were alcoholics and unable to provide for the girls and their three other children (two brothers and a sister), Coreen and Lillian were farmed out in adolescence to other families, while the younger children stayed at home with their parents. Coreen says, "Before we left home, our mother would compare one child with the other in order to build up one's ego. But they would build up one's ego by knocking down the other. So

I spent much of my life hearing things like, 'Coreen's pretty but Lilly's beautiful, and Lilly looks like Elizabeth Taylor.' No matter how I looked I was never going to look good enough, and it was a real sad way to grow up.

"After Lilly and I had been apart and out of touch for so many years, one of us finally decided to pick up the phone. I think it's funny that we really don't recall now which one of us it was; we both were ready, I guess. And although a lot of things had happened over those years, it was as if only a short time had gone by. It was amazing; I was so happy to see her, and I knew I loved her. Children of alcoholics are not taught to love, they are taught to survive; so it was so wonderful for me to feel the deep love that I have for her. It was as if we both had survived it and were going to make it. We both had married, had three children, were divorced. We thought we should try to get our other brothers and sisters together, too, but they wouldn't hear of it. They thought we were really strange. Two of them are very religious now and think of us as awful because we are divorced and Coreen is gay. They just can't believe it. It seems ridiculous that they would allow their notions about lifestyle choice to prevent them from getting to know us their own sisters and discontinue family ties. It's their loss, but it's sad. We all survived the horror of growing up in that hell-house, and now we have the choice to become reconnected, but labels stand in the way."

A. Thomas, S. Chess, and H. Birch have conducted lengthy research into temperament match between mothers and children, and how it can affect sibling relationships. Some babies are slow to warm up to their mother's demonstrations of affection, whereas others are

exuberant and responsive. Children may view this temperament match as favoritism or preference for one
youngster over another.

When I met Suzanne, thirty-three years old and living in
San Francisco, she described her grief over the loss of her
mother, which had occurred just one week before. Unable
to attend the memorial service in the East, she had sent
two poems to be read at the service and a bouquet of her
mother's favorite flowers. "Of all four children," she said,
"I was the only one who really dealt with what Mom
handed out and didn't knuckle under. I was the one she
was proud of for doing that because she always liked a
good fight. She liked me because I was the maverick in the
group, kind of like her."

The rest of the family had always felt ambivalent about
Suzanne because they perceived her as the favorite, and
the fact that she didn't attend the funeral only exacerbated
their antagonism. So they retaliated. "I didn't ask anybody
to read the poems, but it seemed that it would be appropriate," Suzanne told me. "When I called on the day of the
funeral, it seemed like my older sister was really having
her day. I asked about the poems and she said, 'All the
mail hasn't been sorted. Did you send something?' When I
asked to speak to Dad, she said he was eating and didn't
want to disturb him. When I realized what was happening, I felt that I was being excluded from something I
really wanted to dignify with some part of me. It was
awful."

Why did Suzanne let her older sister dictate what would
and would not be allowable at this time? Why did she
regress to the childlike role of allowing her older sibling to
tell her what to do?

This is just one of the many cases illustrating the tremendous capacity for joy *and* heartache in every sisters relationship, and how difficult it is to change family patterns. Denise, thirty-five years old, told me how she yearned for some sympathy from her sister after being rejected by a suitor because she was three years older than he. Her sister's response? "Well, you shouldn't be dating men younger than you anyway. What did you expect?" Peeved, Denise responded, "I thought that for this one time you could begin your response by saying, 'I'm sorry. You must feel awful. I know you liked him a lot.' Save the lecture for the next conversation. Let me just be able to call you for some sympathy." To me, Denise complained, "Why couldn't she just tell me what I needed to hear then? Next time we could have had a discussion about the realities. If I can't rely on my own sister to occasionally indulge my childlike side of whimsy and perhaps fantasy, then who can I rely on? Is that too much to ask?"

Perhaps so. It all depends on the quality of the relationship and what has happened in the past. Karen, twenty-seven years old, handled a similar situation in such a way that she not only got the response she needed, but she taught her sister how to change an old pattern. At the time, she was dating someone her family disliked; her twenty-five-year-old sister, Maggie, who didn't know him very well, couldn't understand the attraction either. Needing to talk out some of her feelings and have Maggie listen uncritically, Karen said to her, "I'm so hard on myself and so self-critical. I want to talk to you about it, but I don't want you to say anything negative. You don't have to lie, but just say the things that you see as positive, or that I could learn from. I really don't want to know that this is something bad. But I could use sitting down and talking with you . . . no judgment."

Maggie felt relieved: "I could see what she needed at that time. I didn't lie, but just for now I agreed not to express my critical feelings. And it was amazing. Once I knew what she wanted, and once she knew I was trying to help her, we had the best talk we have ever had! There weren't these untold silences. I really admire her for telling me exactly what she needed and for letting me have a shot at being supportive."

In another case, a twenty-six-year-old woman, Leigh, who had been molested as a child by her father, and her younger sister, Cindy, were attending a conference. Leigh felt extremely protective of her. Cindy, battling leukemia, and her sister spoke of their pasts and how, eager to leave their parents' home, both had married early, divorced, and were now with men they felt were healthy for them. Leigh said, "But we went through a period of time where there was no relationship at all. And I didn't realize how devastating it could be not to have a relationship with your sister. It can affect everything in your life. Now that we are on a good level again, it is not as though she is a crutch; it is because we are communicating, I know she's there again. I missed her more than I ever missed anyone in my life. And now that we've got some good feelings going between the two of us, I find that I feel that way about almost everything and everyone."

So many sisters let the labels they'd been given in childhood detract from their adult relationship. Consider this from a high-fashion model: "She was always the pretty one and was always on Dad's good side." Never believing that she was prettier than her sister, she chose to "prove it" with her career. Funny, isn't it? Both women could have been models—but the one who chose this career was the "other one."

SHARING

Alex and Shari ended up sharing a room, a closet, and a bureau after their parents divorced. "Sharing a room has always caused a lot of problems," Alex says. "It's always, 'Who's mess is this? It's yours. Who told you you could wear my beige sweater anyway? Look at it, crumpled in a ball and all stretched out.' This caused a lot of hassles between us, and yet in some ways it brought us closer together because when we are lying in bed about to go to sleep we start talking—which we never got to do before because there were a couple of walls between us (physically and emotionally)."

Two sisters, both in their seventies, moved in together after one sister's husband had died. When I met them, they were both widowed and, for the past eight years, had shared everything—shopping, marketing, even going to the dentist. Roxy, the younger sister, described their relationship this way: "When we were younger we didn't get along that well. When we were in grammar school we were both in the same class because I got double promoted. . . . I was a mathematical wiz. I would always give her my test paper when we finished. Then she would give it to our cousin, and all of us girls did real good." The older sister, Dora, remembered, "I was two years older than her and I recall that a man was in our house and he said to my father, 'You know you have a beautiful daughter,' and my father said, 'Oh, you should see my younger daughter. She's smart, and she's good-looking and she's got all the qualifications.' Well, that stayed with me for a long time. Dad loved her more. Our mother thought of me a lot, but Dad preferred her. I recall that after all these years."

CHAPTER 3

HOW FAMILIES LIMIT THE INTIMACY OF THE SIBLING BOND

"My parents were shocked when I entered a marathon because till then they successfully convinced themselves and me that my sister was the 'athletic one.'"

When sisters have problems relating to one another, the difficulties are often rooted in the siblings' dissimilar perceptions of a situation, or in the way the rest of the family has perceived each girl/woman. If we challenge such parentally assigned labels and roles as "the dependable one," "the studious one," "the irresponsible one," or "the self-centered one," sibling conflict is almost inevitable. Even so, it is essential that sisters begin relating to one another as adults, rather than remaining cloaked in these limited identities, which may prevent them from pursuing new careers, new directions—and new selves.

Psychologist Clark Moustakas elaborates on the many

ways that labeling prevents us from getting to know ourselves and other individuals. With everyone—siblings,
too, there is a tendency to focus on the label instead of the
whole person, so that what emerges is a "type" instead of
a multifaceted human. "Labels and classifications make it
appear that we know the other, when actually, we have
caught the shadow and not the substance. In *Individuality
and Encounter: A Brief Journey Into Loneliness and Sensitivity
Groups*, Howard A. Doyle writes: "Since we are convinced
we know ourselves and others . . . [we] no longer actually
see what is happening before us and in not knowing that
we do not know, we make no effort to be in contact with
the real. We continue to use labels to stereotype ourselves
and others, and these labels have replaced human mean-
ings, unique feelings and growing life within and between
persons."

Bossard and Boll list seven general types of roles that
can occur in families:

1. the responsible one
2. the popular, sociable, well-liked one
3. the studious one
4. the self-centered, isolated one
5. the irresponsible one
6. the ill one
7. the spoiled one

Although most of us ascribe negative connotations to
these types, the roles in fact do not *have* to be negative.
Some women report that when their childhood roles are
extended into adulthood, they find them supportive and
comforting. They may discover that the maintenance of an
old role is refreshing in an otherwise constantly changing
environment. Some, however, choose not to change roles
because they are afraid to threaten the family system and

risk upsetting the balance that may have existed for decades.

On the positive side, roles can serve to orient family
members, as well as those outside the family, toward who
does what for whom. But problems tend to arise when at
least one sister feels her persona is defined solely by her
function and she ends up feeling trapped.

But there is ample opportunity in our adult lives to challenge family labels. Because we have the ability and opportunity to develop other aspects of ourselves and our
personalities outside the family, we can become compe-
tent in previously unexplored areas outside our roles.
With sisters, this expansion of life experiences can be both
good and bad. On the one hand, it can be productive for
the woman to discover new aspects of herself and develop
untouched resources. Yet at the same time it can generate
feelings of frustration when her immediate family is not
accepting of her new capabilities. No matter how successful she becomes, parents, brothers, and sisters may still
perceive this woman in the "same old familiar way," and
this tendency is contagious: when she is with her family
the woman herself slips back into the comfortable old self-
image.

But people can change. Leigh and Marta, for example,
were raised to comply strictly with the roles imposed on
them as children. Leigh, the older, more responsible, more
serious one, pursued a career as a music teacher and musi-
cian. Marta, always viewed by her parents as the sociable,
flighty one (they even told her that she "could never hold
a steady job"), traveled, took jobs as they came her way,
and generally did not appear to be in pursuit of any goal.
But, on one of her journeys, Marta met an archeologist
and accepted his invitation to participate in an archeologi-

cal dig. She found this new adventure so exciting that she returned to college to study archeology and became a serious researcher in the field. Before long, she had earned a solid reputation, and for the last five years has worked in a museum.

So you would think that Marta's family would be pleased and proud, wouldn't you? Well, think again. They steadfastly refuse to take Marta's work seriously, consistently trivializing it in family discussions. References to Marta or her work still convey the impression of the irresponsible child frivolously playing with ancient people and their cultures. To the family, Leigh is still the serious one, and there just isn't room for another one like her. Marta persists in trying to break out of the old role in her parents' home, but the more she tries, the more frustrated she becomes, her attempts often humiliating, desperate efforts to maintain her dignity in the face of cynicism and criticism. Ultimately, she learned appropriate ways to communicate her feelings about this treatment to her parents, but until doing so, they thought her outbursts merely proof that she was indeed still a spoiled, self-centered little girl.

Sometimes family roles can be effectively challenged by sisters united in a common front. As children we may not feel we have the tools to challenge our roles, but as adults we can decide whether those roles are appropriate. If the roles coincide with our sibling identity, joining with our sisters can make it easier to challenge them.

Sometimes, women—whether alone or together—find it difficult to challenge family roles, particularly when a role has been assigned to only one sister. The other sister, though not experiencing the role personally, may feel she should just go along with the rest of the family.

Consider the case of Marie. Labeled by her father and, therefore, by the rest of the family, as the "outcast" (to protest would have been tantamount to challenging their father's authority, which just wasn't done), Marie felt unwanted and uncomfortable at home, even around her sister. As a result, she started manifesting unmanageable behavior and was sent to a Catholic boarding school to be "tamed." It was there that Marie experienced love and caring for the first time in her life. She chose to convert to Catholicism and become a nun, but that decision so outraged her father (convincing him that his daughter deserved her outcast status) that he forbade other family members, including Marie's half-sister, from having any contact with her. All of Marie's letters home went unanswered.

Years later, with the girls now adults, Elizabeth went to the convent in search of Marie, hoping to reestablish their relationship. At their reunion, Elizabeth told her older half-sister how she had always admired her and thought of her as a trailblazer and a woman with convictions. Their reconnection was difficult, but when Marie left the convent (at age forty-eight) the two women were finally able to share their feelings with each other.

It took tremendous courage on Elizabeth's part to reestablish contact with her sister, knowing that she was defying her father. Her story reminds me of when *Fiddler on the Roof*'s Tevye forbade four of his daughters from ever contacting the fifth sibling after she married a non-Jew—and they quietly defied him, maintaining secret contact with their "outcast" sister and her new husband. Perhaps the sister's special role in the family as the spirited, independent thinker was one they could not bear to live without.

It is not uncommon for sisters attending my seminars to

discover that one of them wants to change a role pattern that may have started decades before. One sister, Cheryl, announced that she no longer wanted to be the one who always looked after the "difficult arrangements" in the family. If her younger sister, Phyllis, could run a business, she wondered, why couldn't she assume more of the responsibilities for managing complicated family interactions? "You're better at handling Aunt Rose than I am, so *you* call her."

The communication skills required to manage a difficult business client and those required to handle Aunt Rose are very much the same. But perhaps Phyllis avoids the call because the situation conjures up many memories or preset patterns, making the whole interaction seem too restrictive and confining. Asking Cheryl to continue making the calls is her appeal for help. But what happens if Cheryl wants her sister "to deal with her own stuff already"?

What Cheryl and Phyllis do not realize is that a comparison of each other's interpersonal skills is not the issue. What is essential is their relationship with each other and with Aunt Rose. Each of these relationships has its own unique system and set of rules governing the interactions within the system.

In Chapter 8 we will discuss communication rules, but first let's take a closer look at the systems theory. When related parts are rearranged in any system, a change occurs. As William Lederer and Don Jackson point out in *The Mirages of Marriage*, the substance of the whole is determined by all the parts individually, as well as by the way the parts operate in relation to each other. When the system is rearranged in any way (e.g., another person joining it), the system is upset.

Marion, thirty-five, and Stephanie, twenty-five, are sisters in San Francisco who successfully handled a sensitive role transition. Marion is the eldest daughter in a family of eight children. When Stephanie was born, their mother became ill with hepatitis and was unable to care for either Stephanie or the other children. At the age of twelve, Marion became the surrogate mother (not uncommon in large families), as well as the exclusive caregiver. As an adult, Marion chose to remain single, feeling that she had already raised her family. In an attempt to begin her own, independent life she has relinquished the role of "in-house advice giver and mother" by actually removing herself (she has moved to the West Coast).

When Stephanie married, she and her husband were particularly close to Marion. The three of them purchased land together in northern California in the hope of building a "getaway" retreat. When Stephanie's husband was killed in an auto accident two years later, she looked to Marion for support, and once again Marion became the nurturing mother. But because they were not *confined* to those roles in this case, there was little danger that they would become too comfortable in them and unable to give them up. This way it was okay for Marion to be the caretaker—temporarily.

So Marion and Stephanie decided to move in together. They are in the process of creating a home for the two of them, *without* recreating the hierarchical relationship they started with as children. Now they can view each other as adults, as peers. Neither one is always the child or always the mother; each can assume either role when appropriate.

Some sisters expect a certain kind of behavior from their

sibling because it is befitting her role, at least traditionally. Laments like "she should have done this or that because she's the older one . . . she's the younger one . . . she's the one with the special skill" are heard often in my seminars. Leanne, twenty-six, was feeling rather guilty for "leaping ahead of her older sister (Marla)" in her career and personal life. Even though both Leanne and Marla were proud of Leanne's accomplishments, Leanne felt uncomfortable that her big sister was suddenly floundering: "I was getting to the point where I didn't want to tell Marla what was happening because I was so conscious that her life wasn't going well at all. She was unemployed, out of love, and living with our parents while waiting for her luck to change. Then I had to go into the hospital while my parents were away on vacation. Marla was the one who came and got me, took me to the hospital, and then fended off visitors who were tiring me. It was incredibly restorative to me to have my sister in her rightful place, taking care of me and protecting me again. I know it was good for her, too. She needed to be reminded of my vulnerability and my need for her to take care of me, even though it appeared during this time that I was setting the world on fire."

Unfortunately, many women do not tell their sisters what their expectations of each other are, so they are continually being disappointed. Ellen, thirty-eight, and Joan, forty-six, found themselves in such a situation. Ellen's baby daughter had died at five weeks old, but it was not until six years later, at a sisters conference, that she told Joan for the first time that she had never felt the warmth and nurturing she had wanted from her "big sister." Joan was shocked. She couldn't believe that her sister didn't think of her as "being there" for her during her disastrous loss. She felt her role was to keep the family strong and to remind her sister that she, too, had to be strong.

They discussed their family and Joan revealed that she'd had difficulty responding as her sister had wanted be- cause she had yet to finish her own mourning over the loss of their brother, Josh, who had died suddenly when he was sixteen. (Joan was a year younger, and Ellen was nine at the time.) He had been Joan's best friend and she felt the loss terribly. A "tough Bronx kid," she dealt with the loss by getting tougher. She never fully mourned.

So it was all rather simple—and not uncommon. Ellen had internalized the loss of their brother by feeling that she had to replace him in her sister's life. What is impor- tant here is the response (or lack of response) from Joan. For her to identify with her sister when the baby died would have meant she would have had to risk dealing with the unexplored pain of her brother's death, and by insisting that her sister not be allowed to lose control, she protected herself against opening up that wound.

Once they had finally understood some of the "invis- ible" variables at play in the way they communicated, these women were able to clarify their perceptions and expectations of each other and embark upon a more open, loving, and realistic relationship.

Sometimes sisters are unaware that their roles have undergone a transformation. Such was the case with Robin, forty-one, and Jackie, thirty-four. Robin, the eldest of three children and always "the strong one," had re- cently undergone a mastectomy when I interviewed them. Robin said she relied heavily on Jackie during this period, but, even so, she didn't feel that her role as the strong, older sister was in jeopardy.

Jackie, on the other hand, was sensitive to the transformation in their relationship. Having felt all her life like the "baby sister," incapable of doing anything for either her older brother or sister, with this crisis she finally had the sense of being an equal. "I didn't feel like her little sister anymore," said Jackie. "I felt like an equal, someone who she needed for support. For the first time, I felt strong in relation to her, and I believe this has been a turning point in our relationship. In the past, she had never asked me to look after her children, or help her with responsible kinds of things. But now she never hesitates."

Robin looked astonished as she listened to her sister's perception of how her mastectomy had changed their role relationship. Robin had never realized that by allowing her younger sister to take care of her, she had unwittingly helped Jackie develop the confidence to enter into a more egalitarian relationship with her older, more accomplished sister.

But Robin *was* aware of Jackie's strength. "She was a rock for me. My lover crumbled and was scared that I wouldn't be sexually attractive anymore. I think the experience of almost dying, losing a part of my body, and all the rest made me realize how much my sister means to me and what an absolute rock she is. I do depend on her a lot now, and I feel it's okay for me to do that."

Some women need to carve out their own places in the world and decide for themselves which of the role assignments they've carried into adulthood are suitable and which need major restructuring. Janet, a fifty-eight-year-old divorced mother of four grown children, picked up and left her home in Oregon and went to Nantucket Is-

land, Massachusetts, for the winter: "After filling a lot of
roles, I can remember thinking, 'This is my life, you
know!' I was acting like it was somebody else's . . . so-and-
so's wife, and so-and-so's mother, and all of these other
role assignments . . . mother's daughter, Joanne's sister . . ."

Determined to figure out who she would be once she
peeled off all the layers of familial and societal expectations, Janet spent the winter in solitude, writing. "Now
that I am closer to who I think I am than ever before, I am
freer to like my sister, Joanne. And I like her as a person.
She has always been my safety net and still is, but now I
enjoy her and am grateful for her generosity and encouragement without all those old hangups of 'what is expected.'"

Interestingly, Joanne reacted by indicating that she had
never been comfortable with the assigned roles of the past:
"I never felt like the 'safety net'! It was just what I was
supposed to do, to be the one who stayed at home. The
longest time I was ever away from home was when I took
my internship in nutrition in Virginia when I was just out
of college. Then I moved back, got married, and never left
again. I always had tremendous admiration for the fact
that Janet was kind of the mover and the shaker and wrote
fascinating letters; we all lived for the letters that she'd
write home. Everything she has done has seemed to be
more daring and she has always seemed brighter, more
capable and outgoing. I always enjoyed her."

Many women feel the need to find out who they are
under all the layers. Sharon, an accomplished psychologist, writer, teacher, and activist in San Francisco, left
home early to challenge the role and label that had been

hers since childhood: "I was the one who wasn't going to amount to a hill of beans. As a result, I am very achievement oriented, motivated by a desire to break out of the role I was assigned. Unfortunately, I feel very pushy sometimes. I know I push my younger sisters so that they will amount to something; even though they weren't given that obstacle to overcome as I was, it is as if I want to be sure they won't get tangled up in the label that I did."

By establishing her autonomy and identity early on, Sharon actually gained the freedom and confidence to return to her family and establish a new role tailored to *her* specifications.

But it's not only the negative roles that can hinder the development of a healthy sibling relationship. It's very hard to build a trusting relationship with a sibling who perceives you as the "good one," the one who never gets on the parents' bad side. How can you really be an ally?

As we have seen, roles are very often arbitrarily created by a parent, in response to a particular set of family circumstances. Janet, the woman who spent a winter on Nantucket, realizes now that her mother's determination to make her the strong one has left scars; and later on, assigned her sister, Joanne ("the sensitive one"), the task of caring for their aging and infirm mother.

When people become so locked into roles that they feel no freedom and flexibility, they can truly come to believe that they do not have the capacity to assume other, more expanded responsibilities. Jung calls this process "individuation." But as we have seen, people can break out of their roles. Joanne, the "sensitive" and "delicate" one, gradually experienced her own strength while serving as the caregiver to her infirm mother, and thus became the rock on which the family eventually relied. With the passing of years, we each can fill different roles than those assigned to us by our families.

But, of course, not everyone has an easy time being flexible in their assigned roles. When Victoria, a single mother, had two radical mastectomies and, obviously, needed someone to look after her three teenagers, she was unable to go to her younger sister, Tina, because "she had so many psychological problems of her own." Instead, Victoria found the strength within herself and from her solid network of friends. But she would have appreciated her sister's active participation in her life during this crisis: "Relying on my own inner strength was difficult, because I also didn't have someone rooting for me who knew me longer than anyone else in the world. I know Tina was rooting for me in her heart because, since our parents died, she and I were all that was left. But I think it was more because she would have lost her protector and adviser rather than me as a person. It is really tough for me to say that, but five years ago that's how I felt.

"Now things are a little different for Tina. She has gotten a lot of professional help and is out of a terrible marriage, so I think she is learning to rely on herself a bit more. But when I need to talk to someone, although I would love to be able to talk to her and have her help me out, she still thinks of me as the 'infallible' older sister who can't have any problem too big to handle. It really is awful, but I still can't talk to her. I just want her to think of me as human."

That is what most sisters want. But labels and roles are far too often formidable obstacles to the attainment of that goal.

CHAPTER 4

COMMUNICATION—HOW IT HELPS AND HOW IT HURTS

"I pointed out to my sister that my party was formal and she flew off the handle, accusing me of always criticizing the way she looks and her taste in clothes."

Beyond outmoded roles and labels, there are many other obstacles that hinder intimacy between sisters.

One of the major stumbling blocks in this regard is a history of various resentments or preconceived notions that siblings often harbor toward one another, making it difficult for them to freshly reexamine their relationship as they get older. Carrying the emotional baggage of past experience—often inappropriately—they frequently enter situations convinced that more satisfying interactions are impossible.

But if we are to develop more fulfilling relationships with our sisters, we must clear away this old rubble and

63

develop realistic, positive expectations of one another. First you must accept your role in improving the communication interaction. For instance, what aspect of your behavior are you willing to modify to enhance your chances for more successful communication with your sister? In this chapter, we will look at examples of positive and negative interactions in an effort to understand some of the factors contributing to miscommunication. These can serve as an aid in identifying the nuances of detrimental and helpful ways of communicating that may be affecting your ability to get close to your sister.

COMMUNICATION STYLES

Everyone has his or her own "style" of communicating. These styles develop over the years in response to the payoffs connected with them—that is, you learn to interact in a particular way when it has proven useful to you. Your style (or your sister's) can be at once mature, kind, healthy, open-minded, manipulative, deceitful, childlike, bossy, and so on.

For some sisters, their manner of interacting doesn't make either of them particularly happy. And yet they truly feel that they have no alternative methods of relating. Other sisters who are very close feel that they can share their most private selves with each other. They don't need to put on false roles. They know how to communicate with each other, and in some cases (as with many twins), they speak a private language. To each other, their styles are predictable and familiar. Moods are uncannily understood, wordless messages picked up instantly.

This powerful intimacy can provide the foundation for

extremely effective communication. But it has its negative aspects. A major problem may surface, for instance, when the "observing sister" wants to assist the "bothered sister," when the latter doesn't want assistance. In many cases, a troubled woman may just want company, someone she can be herself with without having to talk, or she may just wish to be alone for a while. She may not want her sister to take charge and try to fix things. That spells trouble.

Some sisters have a bleak outlook on the possibility of any future intimacy with their sisters. One woman told me, "She would never understand me. Our lives and purposes are so different. Why should I even try? I see us reenacting the same old stuff we did when we were youngsters." But it is because these women did not offer their true selves to one another, risking confrontation and exposure of their vulnerable sides, that there is this distance between them, often manifested in a properness or a phoniness whenever they are together. "Keeping the peace at all costs" does avoid conflict, but it also keeps the relationship superficial and unsatisfying.

Listen to Janet: "After I found out that our child was severely disabled as a result of birth trauma and some complicating genetic factors, my sister, Grace, came over with a notebook of the names of institutions where we should send Joey. She had researched and discovered everything anyone would want to know about institutional life. The only problem was that neither my husband nor I wanted to send him away! We planned to keep Joey at home with us, utilizing the support services in our area. I understood that Grace's motives were well intentioned, but it really hurt me, for two reasons. First, she just assumed we would send him away. Second, I felt she was rejecting Joey. But instead of saying anything then, I just thanked her. I didn't tell her of our decision at that time because I didn't want her to feel her efforts were futile. I kept thinking that she was just trying to help us out.

"Whenever I get angry at Grace for trying to impose her ideas on us for our child, I try to give her the benefit of the doubt. But the problem is that she has never given up her idea, and whenever she has the chance, she says something like, 'It would be so much easier if you would just send him to an institution, don't you think?' I would love to talk to her about it but I just can't! I have to be so sensitive about her feelings all the time."

Thirty-seven-year-old Dana recently complained to me about the way her older sister, Elena, related to her: "The same obnoxious self comes to the fore whenever we are together. If we shop with one another, Elena never misses an opportunity to tell me that I look too fat and should go on a diet before I buy new clothes. That upsets me. Wouldn't you think she could either not say anything, or perhaps say, 'I know that something is usually bothering you when you gain a few pounds; is everything okay? I'm here if you want to talk.' Why is she always the same selfish person? She's not that way with others, only with me."

Women like Dana see their sisters as being phony to the outside world: "I know who she really is. Who does she think she's fooling?"

Sisters who are close and who feel safe enough with their sisters to be honest and "let their hair down" sometimes do so at the expense of feelings and, to some extent, their relationship. It does not always enhance the sibling bond to throw any barb that might come to mind just to make a point. Such behavior may be perceived by your sister as being "too insensitive" or "too judgmental." Instead, if sisters offer each other the same kind of consideration and insight they give to a friend, the same kind of objectivity and respect, the conflicts over the *context* of the problem—the problem itself—will diminish.

Consider the relationship between Terri, thirty-four, and her sister, Catherine, thirty-seven, who recently spent a quiet weekend together after Catherine's second miscarriage. During the weekend, Catherine talked about her immediate concerns, including her difficulty in getting pregnant and keeping the pregnancy, and her worry about her "biological clock" and her desire for a child. She needed the calming reassurance of a friend, and Terri had seemed like an obvious choice because she, too, had lost her own first baby when she was five months pregnant.

Initially, Terri had not been supportive of Catherine's efforts to become pregnant, because she had thought that Catherine was taking too much of a physical risk. Years earlier, she had tried to influence Catherine to have her children when she was younger, before she had established her professional life. But Catherine had decided to wait, and now, although she did not regret her decision, she needed to discuss its ramifications with someone she trusted, someone other than her husband.

Fortunately, Terri proved to be the perfect choice. She listened actively and empathetically. She became a sounding board for Catherine's questions, tears, and convictions. By the end of the weekend, Catherine was sure she had found a friend in her sister—a nonjudgmental, reassuring listener who would ease the decision-making process for her.

*   *   *

Let's take a closer look at the process of communication. In their book *The Pragmatics of Human Communication*, Paul Watzlavick, Janet Beavin, and Don Jackson discuss the messages we give each other in terms of the content of the message and the relationship itself. This approach not only facilitates interpretation of the content, but also provides us with considerable information about how we see the other person, how we see ourselves, what kind of a relationship the two of us have in this particular situation, and what we can look for in the future.

On at least three occasions, we are keenly aware of relationship messages: first, when, in a given situation, the message seems to drastically violate our expectations for the relationship; second, when we are involved in relationships with high levels of intensity; and third, when disagreement and conflict arise.

Along these lines, many of us tend to get caught up in the "analogic" aspects of communication, paying closer attention to *how* something is said than *what* is said. "I'd be better able to take my sister's advice if she offered it a bit more gently, a bit more kindly," one woman told me. "If she spoke to her friends the way she speaks to me, she wouldn't have any friends! I don't want her to be phony, though I would like a bit more consideration." Albert Mehrabian, a psychologist who specializes in the field of nonverbal communication, noted that in the situations he and his colleagues examined only 7 percent of the impact of communication was verbal; the remaining 93 percent was nonverbal. Body language is a powerful nonverbal form of communication. A simple shrug of the shoulders or lift of an eyebrow can eloquently convey a woman's feelings about her sister.

Too often, however, what sisters *hope* to communicate

may not be what is indeed communicated. When your sister says something, you may almost reflexively react the same way you did when you were a teenager, perhaps because you heard in her tone something reminiscent of the days when you were both on the cheerleading squad, for instance. Rather than responding to *what* was being said (the content portion of the message), you may respond to *how* it was said (the relationship portion of the message), or how you *think* it was said.

This explains in part why, for many of us, no matter how sophisticated we are, our sisters can "get to us" as no other person can. To a sister, an event in adulthood can remind her of how her sibling acted, looked, or responded many years before, when they were nearly inseparable.

Of her sister a woman named Sue said, "She ate every meal with me, knew each of my teachers' names, knew how well I tap-danced, knew when I fell off a horse, and knew when my feelings were hurt by some wisecracking kid in the neighborhood. She either comforted or jabbed me at each of those times. Back then, it appeared that her friends were the all-important people in her life, and that I was always 'in the way.' I remember watching her first teenage party in the basement from the stair landing in my best clothes. I forfeited my teddy bear because I wanted to look mature enough in case one of the boys asked me to dance. I had spent the whole afternoon practicing the newest steps just in case. Even though I had promised my sister that I wouldn't bother them, I hoped that one of the boys would see me and ask me to dance. It didn't happen.

"What I still cannot understand is, if I was so busy getting 'out of the way, out of her hair, out of her room, out of her closet, out of her diary,' when did she notice so much of what was happening to me that she can recall it all so readily now? Can it be that in those days my every move was recorded indelibly in her mind so that she could use it as a referent or ammunition to tattle or to support? And if she does know everything, why is there often such difficulty communicating?"

One possible answer to this question, of course, has already been advanced—namely, that each of us views our own specific communication interactions from an experienced yet biased perspective. Sisters who grew up together have a sense of each other's history and series of experiences, but they rarely have the same *perception* of these events and people. So, although you and your sister may have shared much of your histories, your perception and memories are *not* the same. Nobody can see a situation exactly as someone else sees it.

As you might imagine, this can create a fundamental problem in communication. It will be hard for you to communicate effectively with your sister if you believe that your perceptions and hers match. After all, if you think that way, in an argument how will you be able to see a situation from her perspective? What would be the point?

This inability to conceptualize another perspective inevitably leads to the complaint "You may have heard that, but it is not what I said." Often sisters "mind-read," assuming they know what their sister is thinking or feeling, not only finishing their sentences verbally, but anticipating in their heads what is to come—constructing a reply or a solution to a problem when it is the act of sharing, not the finding of a solution, that is valuable.

Of course, many sisters feel a special connection with their sisters. They point out how, without planning, they will wear the same clothes, choose the same greeting cards, or call one another just because they had a feeling that the other needed to talk. But when conflict occurs, they may not be able to employ this mind-reading skill. It is during these times of conflict that they need to listen to their sisters more than ever, rather than second-guessing them.

ENHANCING COMMUNICATION SKILLS

In order to improve communication with your sister on all levels, it is essential to remember that she is no longer a little girl, and that she has a life of her own, separate from her life with you. When she states whatever is on her mind, there are a variety of possible motives: she may simply be making conversation; she may be trying to feel connected to you; or she may actually want your opinion on something. Try to understand her motivation. Perhaps in the past you have been impatient with her tardiness in getting to the point. Maybe she talks in circles, and you have often cut her off, leaving her feeling that you are rushing her and/or are not interested in what she has to say. Rather than continuing this pattern, be specific with her about how you would like her to focus on what is on her mind. Or learn to adjust to *her* style, become more patient, and try to listen to what she has to say.

But sometimes a sister's style is just too difficult for you to deal with. In that case, call a meeting and try to explain your concerns to her. Begin with *your* perceptions, noting that you see the communication between the two of you as faulty and lacking. Explain that you know things could be better, that you are willing to make the effort to improve things between you, and that you would like to hear her thoughts about the situation.

Many women complain that their sisters simply don't listen to them. Consequently, I tell women that it is important for them to evaluate their ability to listen. When your sister says something and you think you understand what is said, then paraphrase it—repeating it to her in your own words, emphasizing the content. This simple procedure can prevent countless misunderstandings.

Paraphrasing involves restating the essence of what was said. It should always be concise, never any longer than the original statement. (If the paraphrase is too long, the sister who began the discussion can get caught up in the exchange and lose her train of thought.) The paraphrase should focus directly and explicitly on the substance of the statement, not on the aspects of the relationship that may be determining the manner in which it's stated. Deal with the facts, and how you think your sister feels, *not how you feel while hearing what has just been said.* What is essential is your ability to accurately identify your sister's ideas and feelings—her emotional state. Be sure you paraphrase her statement in your own words, so that as she looks at the situation from her sibling's perspective, she can see that you, too, bring a unique viewpoint to the subject.

Why do I stress the importance of including emotion as well as content? Because not understanding or responding to a sister's emotional state is one of the most common complaints I hear from sisters: "I just don't think she has any idea how I feel."

It's no surprise, with all the opportunities for misunderstandings, that many people have difficulty sharing their innermost feelings with their sisters. Most often, women explain that they fear their feelings will not be validated or accepted, and they do not want to risk making themselves vulnerable to criticism from someone who has the power to hurt them so deeply. Too often, sisters believe that the old labels will come hurtling back at them if they open themselves up—and that they will once again be the "younger, inexperienced, immature, and incompetent one," or the "experienced, never-frightened older sister," or the "indecisive, wishy-washy" sister of years ago.

But what about the other side of that coin? A woman who allows herself to be vulnerable to hurt also opens herself up to the more positive, joyful feelings her sibling may be expressing. Sisters *can* become more emphatic listeners, more accepting of one another, but until they do, there is this feeling that something special is missing.

To resolve such problems, I suggest that you be aware of your sister's feelings. Rather than ignore her emotional state because you are protecting yourself from being vulnerable, take a risk. Respond. Say things like, "That must be frustrating for you," "That's terribly disappointing," "That's thrilling!" And listen very carefully for the "feeling" words (*ignored, left out, foolish, relieved, worried, trapped, happy, peaceful, energetic*). These can help you see beyond your sister's words, to her emotional state. Be assertive in conveying *your* emotional state. Ask yourself, "What would I be feeling if I were the one saying and doing these things?" Tell your sister the answer. Everyone is unique, but just by trying to experience your sister's feelings, you have a better chance of encouraging her to be more open—now and in the future. The next time you come to her for help, you may very well receive a more empathic response.

Discouraging the disclosure of feelings not only separates the listener from the speaker's feelings, but distances the speaker herself from what is prompting her to speak. By encouraging your sister to express her personal feelings, you can help her better understand her own emotional state, thereby enabling her to get closer to a solution—and, in fact, closer to her *self.* Many women feel that they are supposed to "solve" their sister's problems for them; but actually what is most often needed is someone who will listen to what we are saying, help us look at the elements of the problem, sometimes offering suggestions that would be consistent with our own personal style.

There are times, however, when we can go a step further and communicate to your sister what you think she feels, as well as your best guess as to *why* she may feel that way. For example: "You feel irritated because mother won't treat you as an adult and as if you can't make up your own mind." In most cases, sisters not only want their sibling to receive their communication accurately, but they also seek warmth and concern. This is one way to demonstrate that reception. Your compassion will help your sister feel less alone—whatever the problem.

Even if you don't now consider yourself a great listener—or if your sister has sometimes told you, "You never hear what I am saying to you"—you can begin making a conscious effort to improve your listening skills. That doesn't mean faking it; when you don't understand what she has said, either because it was too complicated, or because you got sidetracked, be honest. "I seem to have missed something" is a much better response than scrambling to catch up and put pieces together that may not be there. It is usually more effective to say, "Please say that again a different way," rather than "I know what you mean"—when in reality you're not at all sure that you understand the message. Try saying, "I was following you all the way until you mentioned Michael, and then I lost you. Would you please go over what happened after that point?"

Even after you feel confident that you are following what is going on, and you have done a few paraphrases just to be certain, avoid telling your sister that you "know just how she feels." Nobody ever knows "exactly" how someone else feels, and a sister may respond to a remark like that by shutting up or biting back. ("You do not!") Why such a violent reaction? Intrinsic to the sisters relationship is the need to separate, and very often there has been a prolonged attempt by each sister to maintain a boundary around her own identity—much like the line down the middle of the car seat that outlined my sister's and my territories on those family outings! Sisters want their private feelings to be distinct, and even though a woman trusts her sister enough to share feelings with her, it is vital that her feelings remain just that—*her* feelings. Yes, of course you may be able to empathize, but your feelings are simply not the *same* as your sister's, and it's damaging to both of you to convince yourselves otherwise.

Becoming an attentive, reflective, and helpful listener takes time. Few problems are solved overnight. When one sister doesn't take the time to listen to what is being said by the other, to reflect back and comment, time may be saved, but the relationship may suffer greatly. Whenever we do not listen to what is being said to us, whenever we do not show a deep concern for the *essence* of a specific problem, our efficiency for relating to our sister is greatly reduced, our chances for true intimacy lessened.

CHAPTER 5

WHY PARENTS PERPETUATE OLD PATTERNS

"My father insists that he cannot talk to my sister; he stopped trying about five years ago. I get put in the middle, and now that I think about it, he has no reason to talk to her because I transmit all of the news between them!"

Sisters are not the only ones who may perpetuate a destructive pattern in their relationship. Parents, too, often have an investment in keeping the family system the way it is—even if it means undermining the bonds between their offspring. Some parents give mixed messages; they are ambivalent about whether they really want their children to be close, because they fear that if their children do strengthen their bonds *they* will no longer be "needed," or their own position in the family will be threatened. Some sisters find they are only able to develop closer ties with each other and shatter old childhood patterns *after* their parents have died.

This need not be the case. You can change without divorcing yourself from your parents. But it does require a change in the way you respond to your parents and/or sister.

Think about the way you communicate with your parents. Perhaps you tend to talk only about each other—whether it's on the phone or in person. Your dialogues may perpetuate the very labels, myths, and roles that isolate you from your sister. Try to expand the focus of these "family news" conversations to include other aspects of your life—although of course certain subjects can still remain off limits. Acceptable topics for discussion are: work, travel, friends, and ideas about the world, such as politics, fashion, trends in thinking.

But you must be careful about the manner in which you enlarge the scope of your conversations. Many parents interpret this as a sign that *all* personal aspects of their children's lives are fair game. Unless they know "everything," they are not content. As a daughter with a life of your own, you may very well feel uncomfortable—justifiably so—talking to your mother about every aspect of your personal life. You may even feel guilty about your desire to keep "private areas" to yourself, and your parents may capitalize on that. When one adult woman would not tell her sixty-year-old mother about her social life, the older woman complained, "But I told my mother *everything!* Why do you have such secrets? I feel as if I am the last to know everything. I learn about your activities from neighbors or your sister."

To that mother—who was raised by immigrant parents in a small apartment, and who spent the first few years of

married life either living with them or within walking distance—there was no such thing as "personal news."
Everybody knew everything! "I just want to be a part of
her life," this mother said. "Is that such a crime?" To her
daughter, it isn't exactly a crime—but it is an intrusion,
and the daughter still has a problem setting limits with her
mother when it comes to revealing aspects of her personal
life.

Sometimes mothers use the rivalry inherent in the sisters relationship to their advantage: "I can communicate
with your sister. So it's not me—it must be *you!* Why are
you so difficult to talk to?" This kind of comment serves
only to drive whatever wedge already exists between two
sisters even deeper. Perceived favoritism that began in
childhood can be reactivated by the mother's presentation
of which daughter she feels "closer" to and can most easily
talk to.

As you might imagine, this kind of manipulation can
put sisters in a very uncomfortable position. A woman
may begin to worry that her sister might tell their mother
and father some of her secrets. And when parents—for
whatever reason—use one daughter to find out information about the other, or pit one against the other, they may
be perpetuating patterns and roles that the sisters have a
hard time challenging.

Consider Donna, age thirty-eight, married and the
mother of three, who talks to her mother, Mimi, on the
phone once a week. Invariably, Mimi asks Donna about
her younger sister Joelle's social life: Was Joelle seeing anybody? Did she talk about one man more than any other?
What did Donna think Joelle would do with her life?

Donna became increasingly irritated. She felt she was

being manipulated into gossiping about her sister and she wanted to tell her mother that she felt uncomfortable whenever she was asked questions about Joelle. She decided that she could no longer allow herself to be in the middle, and she began inventing excuses to end telephone conversations early or to avoid questions. Realizing that she had become unpleasant and abrupt, she decided instead to tell her mother directly that she wasn't going to be the informer on Joelle's life anymore; if Mimi had inquiries about Joelle, she would have to ask Joelle directly.

Donna and her mother needed a new, stronger base for their relationship. It was no longer acceptable for Donna to be the primary information link between her sister and her mother, and it was time for Donna to tell her mother so, emphatically and firmly.

The ramifications of this "go-between" situation extended beyond the mother-daughter relationship. Donna found that these conversations interfered with her relationship with Joelle. Having come to think of Donna as a "spy," Joelle began their conversations with, "Let's just keep this between us," or "Don't tell Mom this"—just as she had when they were children, keeping "sisterly secrets." And, in fact, she began keeping a few secrets from Donna—things she would gladly have shared with her sister before. Clearly, the trust between Donna and Joelle—essential in any close relationship—was disintegrating.

When Donna explained to her mother that she had begun to dread their conversations, anticipating at every moment the inevitable query about Joelle, her mother said she didn't think it was a problem, since she and Donna could "talk like sisters," while she and Joelle had a more formal, "distanced" relationship. She added, "Any mother likes to know about her daughter's life. So please drop the subject."

Donna was far from satisfied with this response, and she did raise the issue again, the next time more succinctly, warning that even if her mother insisted on asking about Joelle, she simply would not discuss it. She added that, although she hoped this would not hinder their closeness, she couldn't fully accept their relationship as it stood now. Donna reassured her mother that she loved her very much and felt confident that they could proceed with their relationship—excluding comments about her sister's personal life.

Like all parents, Donna and Joelle's mother had certain expectations for her daughters. Early on, these expectations—implicit and explicit—often center around how the parents' lives will be different, who they are as parents, what their children will be like as individuals, and how they will relate to their siblings; and children's sensitive antennae invariably pick them up.

How many of you remember the jumble of feelings evoked when parents said, "When I come from the hospital, I'll bring you a present—a baby. You will love her, she'll be someone fun to play with, and you will be such good friends"? Many parents cherish the notion that siblings exist to love, protect, and share with each other—in addition to being best friends. Whether expressed verbally or nonverbally, consciously or unconsciously, children sense and very often define their roles as siblings in terms of these adult expressions.

From childhood, we are told that a "good sister" does this, a "bad sister" does that, and many parents continue to intervene in the sisters relationship into adulthood.

When mothers try to involve themselves in their daughters' discussions, their offspring complain, "If only my mother would leave us alone and not intrude, I could be nicer to my sister." Joan, forty-six, a successful business executive, said, "I feel as if Mother wants my sister and me to be friends so much that if we have an argument in her presence, she always interferes. It's just like when we were children. We weren't allowed to fight. Whenever we did argue, and one of our parents heard, they would cut in and say, 'Sisters who love each other don't fight; now make up with each other and tell her you love her right now.' Then and now, it's been like having a referee! Mother still reminds me that I should be nicer to Sherry because she never had it as easy as I did. I am sick of hearing that. I have heard it since I was a child—and the way I remember, I didn't have it so easy!"

Whenever Joan and Sherry do or say *anything* that reminds their mother of the way they acted as children, their mother points this out as though it were history repeating itself, with much of the focus on former bad habits. Now Sherry and Joan have decided just to laugh about it. "Sometimes, though," Joan says, "I have to admit, I still get a knot in my stomach when Mom or Dad pulls one of these reminders. I guess I have to work on that."

The concept of "working on that" is addressed in a book by psychiatrists Harold Bloomfield and Leonard Felder, *Making Peace with Your Parents*. In their view, many unresolved conflicts like Donna's and Joelle's become obstacles to the attainment and maintenance of positive relationships between all members of the family.

In *My Mother, My Self* Nancy Friday explores her own family dynamic, outlining how she gradually became aware of her feelings of competition toward her mother and her overwhelming jealousy toward her sister, Susie. Unaware of the tremendous motivating influence of these feelings throughout her teenage years, as an adult she gradually came to see their pervasive role, and now she claims that her self-sufficiency was due, in great part, to her jealousy of Susie. Susie was always considered the beauty in the family, and Friday remembers feeling that their mother couldn't take her eyes off her. To this day, the two sisters have a distant relationship, in part as a result of the distinct way each was "parented."

Chantal, age twenty-seven, an accomplished fitness instructor and prize-winning body builder, experienced similar problems with her sister, Suzette, thirty. They were both raised in France until their mid-teens. Suzette began winning beauty contests when she was twelve, and her mother and father used to remark constantly about her extraordinary looks. Today, whenever Chantal and Suzette plan to get together, Chantal pointedly informs Suzette about her next competition—clearly her only card in a family deck that she feels is stacked against her. But whenever her sister and mother do plan to attend one of Chantal's competitions, she pulls a muscle and cannot compete. One can only assume that this is related to the insecurities she carries into adulthood from their parents' "bias" toward Suzette.

In *The Body Has Its Reasons*, Therese Bertherat and Carol Bernstein emphasize the connection between physical and emotional pain. At seminars, interviews, and informal discussions I too am impressed with the apparent physical manifestations of a sister's resentment toward a sibling who she feels is a burden. Such expressions as "carrying resentment around" typify the manner in which we internalize feelings about our families. Resentment makes its presence known in a variety of physiological symptoms. "You're driving me crazy," "You're a pain in the neck," "Whenever I see you, my stomach ties up in knots"—all are potent descriptions of how we feel, literally and figuratively.

But time, so it is said, brings change, and, although in the past we may have perceived our sisters as "real pains," they rarely stay in that "painful" stage forever. Then why do we continue to respond to them in the "old" way? Very often it's because we have not learned alternative ways of dealing with them. I am constantly amazed by sisters at the seminars who seem to be unaware that, as adults, they can change the way they relate to their brothers, sisters, and parents.

Jana and Brenda are sisters who have tried and succeeded in relating to each other more positively as adults. They live near each other, talk often, and whenever they find themselves falling back into their "established patterns," one of them jokingly mimics their parents. Immediately, they see how ridiculous they had been acting, and they are able to return to their adult selves.

Jana and Brenda have hit upon a formula for maintaining closeness. Obviously, this is not the kind of technique most of us could use as children, and our parents may never have acquired appropriate tools or techniques to promote positive parent-child and sister-sister relationships. But there's no point blaming them; it's up to you to rely on your own skills, to generate new options by considering the issue on a one-to-one basis with your sister.

Suzanne's case illustrates what happens when a sister learns new interpersonal skills. The youngest in a family of three sisters, all now in their thirties, she experienced tremendous sibling rivalry while growing up. She described her mother as an intense woman who clung to the fantasy of her daughters as being consistently loving and supportive—oblivious to the reality of the situation, which was that they had actually caused each other a great deal of pain.

A year prior to our conversation, Suzanne's mother had died after a long illness that had caused mental and physical deterioration. "During the time she was ill," Suzanne said, "on my many visits to Seattle where she lived, it became apparent to me and my sisters that the three of us were getting along better than we had ever gotten along before. Although throughout our lives my mother sincerely had wanted us to be close, it was at the time of her last illness that we experienced more love and good feelings than we did when she was sharp and active. It seems strange that even though she wanted us to be close, she was responsible for establishing a pattern in which there was a lot of in-fighting and jealousy."

Suzanne shared this perception with her sisters at one of their dinners together during this period: "Maybe I'm just imagining this, but I feel much warmer toward all of you. There seems to be less antagonism and conflict between us." One of her sisters attributed this to the fact that "Mom's not on the phone pitting us against one another, because she's not mentally able to do that anymore." Suzanne felt pleased that as sisters they were finally able to relate to each other in the way their mother had envisioned—and yet sad that it took her death to bring them together.

What had Suzanne's mother done wrong? Despite her apparent desire for the girls to be supportive of each other, she didn't know how to establish ground rules for them to do so. She was unable to set an example for them. After she died, her children no longer could use her as a reference point for their self-validation: "Are we good yet, Mom? Am I the one who shines in this threesome?" Without their "anchor," they became free simply to enjoy each other without jealousy.

Unlike Suzanne and her sisters, there are women who never look back at their childhood experiences as a series of *past* events; they can't separate these situations from their adult lives. For these people, the often devastating experiences of childhood—such as being raised by abusive or unfit parents—accompany them throughout their adult lives. Earlier I referred to two daughters of alcoholic parents who, in remembering their childhoods, commented that they were not taught to love—they were taught to survive—and it was only after they had learned the appropriate "survival skills" that they then felt the need to love. When parents interfere in the process of learning to love, sisters may have to turn to each other for the necessary support and compassion.

For forty years, Rochelle, fifty-six, has been estranged from her family. As a child she was severely "disciplined" by her father, and she resented her sister Dana for not coming to her defense more often. As often occurs in abusive families, Rochelle was singled out as the "target child" (targeted for abuse) and was unable to understand what she had done that so enraged her father. Whenever her sister came to her aid, her father sent Dana away. Soon Dana stopped protesting altogether, and Rochelle was left to fend for herself.

Rochelle attended a recent sisters seminar alone. Describing her many mixed feelings for Dana, she said she felt a tremendous void whenever she spoke of her estranged sister, and she had come to the seminar to try to gain some insight into the roles her sister and her father still played in her life. As an adult, Rochelle had always been reluctant to contact her sister because their father lived with Dana and her family. Although she expressed no remorse for not contacting her father, she wanted to be able to contact Dana without her father's knowledge.

Rochelle focused first on improving her own physical and emotional health by joining a support group and beginning a regular program to manage stress. As time passed, she felt ready to send Dana an audio tape. In it she told her how often she thought of her, and she asked if Dana ever thought of their childhood together, and she said she was interested in hearing from her. She stated emphatically, however, that she was *not* interested in establishing any contact with their father. That was her only "condition." Dana wrote back, asking that she reconsider—apparently their father was dying. But Rochelle was not yet ready to deal with her father, and she reiterated her desire to renew contact with Dana alone. They did reestablish a connection, and at the time of this writing are planning a visit. It will be their first in forty years.

As Rochelle discovered, carrying around hatred for or disappointment in one's parents can hinder other relationships. But to strengthen a sibling bond, you have to be ready to deal with ancient, and hitherto unexplored, pains from childhood. And resentment toward your parents for putting barriers up between you and your sister only makes things more difficult.

Seminar attendees have remarked that it is usually easier to deal with parental issues separately from sister issues because, taken together, they can be confusing. As you will find, what you feel was done to you as a youngster need not have the same force and control over you as an adult. You are no longer a child, subject to the pains and confusions of your family. Remember, the past is over.

As you progress, keep your expectations for your parents and your sisters realistic. They will probably not change their behavior. Resenting them now for not taking care of your needs many years ago probably will not rehabilitate them. However, if you want an improved, adult relationship, your *response* to them can—indeed, *must*—change.

Look to others for meeting your needs. Increase the size of your "family" by expanding your definition of the word. Consider friends as family. Those sisters in my seminars who have successfully done this have said they feel more at peace with their families and their parents in particular.

Two such sisters, Betty, thirty-one, and Wendy, thirty-three, live three thousand miles apart. As they were growing up, Wendy was the more independent one, whereas Betty was the daughter who always followed in her mother's footsteps, winning the "good girl" label. Betty describes Wendy as a "typical middle child" (they have an older brother): "Wendy was always left out, kind of dumb, never having her own opinions even though she was an individual. She tried to be good but never was quite good enough. My brother and I could intimidate her incredibly well and we did so at every opportunity. Our mother never believed her and we knew it. We took advantage of it, too. When all three of us kids fought, or when we had different versions of a story, we were all put into a room together until we came up with one version of the story. And it was usually our version, not Wendy's."

Bruce, the oldest sibling, was as strong-willed as Betty.

Wedged between these two powerful personalities, Wendy didn't have a chance. All she wanted was to get away. During their "problem-solving sessions" she would always concede, even if her version of the story was correct. She began to feel she could not trust her parents to believe anything she said.

Despite her chronological age—and because of her confidence—Betty assumed the role of the older sister, an act encouraged by her mother because, after all, everyone knew that Wendy "could not be trusted to make the right decisions." In fact, Wendy's impulsive nature had always reminded her mother of the children's father, a fact that she continually brought up during any disagreement. And since their mother ran the household, it was better to be like her than like their father.

Betty, on the other hand, didn't fight with their mother because, she was told, they were so much alike; she was not just a daughter—she was a friend. Thus, Wendy grew up with the feeling she was missing something special: "Mom related to me differently. She always told me I didn't listen, even though I did. I listened real hard, it's just she used to repeat the same thing over and over. To this day, mother tells me fewer things because she thinks I am not bright enough to understand what's she's saying. It's amazing how she won't give up her view of me as the one who is slower."

This pattern was perpetuated by the entire family. As children, Betty was the perfect, wonderful kid who would go to great lengths to make her sister look stupid so that she would appear bright. Wendy, always told by her siblings that she was dumb, did poorly in school and decided she might as well pursue her own life, outside of the family, using her own and other nonfamily opinions of herself to gauge her talents.

But the adult world plays funny tricks on people. Betty discovered that, in reality, she may not have actually been as independent as Wendy. Indeed, Wendy never searched for parental approval. Since it seemed unattainable, she was happiest making her own decisions, without her parents' approval or knowledge—buying her wedding dress without her mother, living with a younger man, taking a job without first discussing it with her parents. But she wasn't behaving out of defiance; she was doing what she needed to do to feel good about herself.

Today the sisters get along well with each other. Wendy doesn't resent or feel threatened by Betty or Bruce and lives by the rule "Let's not gossip about anyone in the family." When her mother tries to comment on her decisions, judgments, or choices, Wendy merely listens. The maternal "commentary" about her wisdom (or lack thereof) no longer bothers her. She now addresses any derogatory comments as soon as they are mentioned, before her anger escalates the matter, thereby preserving her own self-esteem and, in so doing, her relationship with her parents.

Just as learning to express yourself with your parents without forfeiting your self-esteem is critical, so is the development of skills for accepting your parents and sisters as they are. This does not mean you can't help them break old patterns—by your own response to them you can. But you must be quite sure of exactly what it is that you want from them.

Think about it. Are you absolutely certain you are ready to give up the way you have related to your parents for so

long, and vice versa? Jane, forty-five, and Marilyn, forty-
one, still find their mother and father talking to them as if
they were teenagers when they come home. According to
Jane, who usually occupies center stage in the family, "It's
interesting to watch how my parents try to include Marilyn in the conversation. They don't expect her to be interested, so they usually ask for her agreement, rather than
for any original ideas. Just like when we were younger,
she usually feigns being tired and goes to another room.
What's interesting is that I usually don't realize this is
happening until it is too late. I am so used to this behavior
occurring in that house. It's like when we walk into the
house and are surrounded by those walls, we become
teenagers again, responding to our parents in the way we
were trained."

Sifting through conflicting parental expectations can
make a child's search for his or her own goals and values
an extremely confusing endeavor. This is a particularly
timely theme today, with so many women choosing
careers over marriage and children, thereby confounding
traditional parental expectations. Christine, thirty-four,
went to graduate school in sociology and pursued a career
as a college professor. She was involved in the university
community and became a role model for her students as
she enjoyed a life of research, teaching, and public speaking. By many persons' standards, she lived a well-
balanced and integrated life.

Christine's sister, Maxine, thirty-one, had also been a
schoolteacher and tutored part time in her home. She, too,
felt she had a well-balanced, integrated life. Both of the
sisters were extremely happy, respected each other's
choices, and stayed in touch with one another. Christine

reveled in her role as the "doting aunt" and helped with child care whenever possible.

The problems arose at family gatherings. Christine's parents would usually ask her about work and would then turn their attention to the grandchildren. Implicitly and explicitly, they gave Christine the message that they saw her life as "incomplete," "unfulfilled," and "selfish" because she had not "settled down" and given them more grandchildren. Maxine became the favored child, and Christine realized that no career, no lifestyle, could win her that prized position.

Both Christine and Maxine realized that neither of them could ever make their parents appreciate different lifestyles. To their parents, a career was nice on the side, but marriage and children were the only options.

Another important issue in the context of parents' expectations and the perpetuation of old patterns is illustrated by the case of Nettie, twenty-nine. Slated to become the lawyer in the family, her parents had encouraged her not to marry young. But, although she was extremely bright, she couldn't seem to pass the state bar exam.

After Nettie's fifth try at the bar, her sister, Eleanor, twenty-five, stepped in and explained to her parents that they were putting too much pressure on Nettie, that in fact her whole sense of worth within the family had come to rest upon whether or not she would become a lawyer. Eleanor encouraged her parents to ease up on her sister. Since Nettie herself had not spoken up—she felt incapable of fighting this formidable family conspiracy—she took Eleanor's intervention as a heartening sign of support.

Annie, forty-three, is the mother of four teenagers and a part-time student who works outside her home. Her business schedule leaves little time to even consider restructuring her relationship with her parents: "For ease, I'd just rather leave it the way it is and not upset the applecart. I find it interesting, though, that my sister has so much time to 'work on' her relationship with each member of the family. I'd rather live, not think about living."

Two weeks after she said this, Annie wrote me a letter indicating her ambivalence about her sister's commitment to the family. She wondered whether her reluctance meant that she just didn't care that much about her sister and her parents and she feared she was setting a bad example for her own children.

The parental relationship is a complex one—difficult, but not impossible to change. By now you should be able to recognize some of the elements that may be playing a role in your interactions with your own parents. As some of the examples have shown, improvement in this fundamental relationship has helped many women feel more fulfilled and complete in other areas of their lives.

CHAPTER 6

SISTERS, HUSBANDS, AND LOVERS

"When my sister decided to marry Mark she gave me the greatest compliment. She said, 'He brings out all the parts of me that, till now, only you have been able to bring out.' "

Most women fantasize about their sisters marrying "Mr. Right" and living "happily ever after." Similarly, men often recognize the importance that a sisterly relationship can play in their wives' lives, and thus believe that this sibling bond deserves to be nurtured. Even so, this male "third person" who enters the sisters' arena is as frequently a source of sibling stress as sibling strength.

It may seem ideal when two sisters are able to connect on a basic, feeling level; but, in fact, in this scenario "significant others" like a husband or a lover often feel threatened. It can be a tremendous assault to his masculinity that "I can't be all things to her." And he may wonder, "Why can you tell her and not me?" or "Are you telling her our secrets?" The jealousies of husbands and lovers can become wedges driven between sisters.

As for the sisters themselves, they often say they are willing to accept certain behavior from a brother-in-law that they would not accept from anyone else, because they don't want to ruin their own sibling relationship. But if they choose instead *not* to tolerate this offensive behavior, they place their sibling bond in jeopardy by leaving their sister with the feeling that she has to choose between her sister and her husband.

Margaret and Jennifer enjoyed each other immensely. Not only did they live together, but they also shared the after-hours of their very different lifestyles. Everything was perfect . . . until Joel entered Margaret's life. To Jennifer, he seemed insensitive and remote. Unlike most of her sister's previous beaux, Joel did not appear the least bit interested in getting to know Jennifer, and overall he didn't seem like the kind of man either of them would want to live with. Three months later, Margaret announced they were engaged, and Jennifer was crushed. This was certainly not the brother-in-law *she* had hoped for, and she wondered whether her sister would be happy with this man.

But Jennifer said nothing. The future made her particularly ill at ease. Would she "fit into" their lives? Would she still be welcome to drop by, have dinner, go to a museum or a show with Margaret on the spur of the moment? It was bad enough that her sister was being taken away from her. Why did the perpetrator have to be someone who seemed so foreign?

Jennifer interpreted her future brother-in-law's abruptness as a form of verbal abuse. Yet she kept silent, and in the ensuing years much of the lives of these sisters went unshared. When Margaret began having "normal marital problems" she did not feel comfortable telling Jennifer about it because she sensed her sister's disapproval of Joel. Jennifer, on the other hand, continued to pretend there were no problems, at the same time never making any great effort to get to know her brother-in-law on his terms. Perhaps he would have rejected her attempts, but she never even tried. She took an egocentric, defeatist attitude, assuming stubbornly that since he didn't fit into her model, and didn't communicate the way she wanted him to, there was no chance for them to become close. Perhaps Jennifer felt that if she tried to get to know him by playing by his rules she would, in some way, become like him. Since she perceived him as mighty and powerful, she may have felt that she would not be able to maintain her sense of self and her own style and would be swallowed up by him.

As it turned out, once Jennifer had become surer of herself and more confident in her interpersonal skills, she was finally able to accept Joel as he was without measuring him up against impossible standards. But that occurred years later. Her life and Margaret's life would have been enriched had she been able to do this earlier. Had she accepted that Margaret must have seen something wonderful in this man and, as her sister and most fervent admirer, tried to discover those qualities too, their relationship could have grown even closer. But Jennifer had pulled farther and farther away over the years, convinced that she was right, and that he was a cool, proud man who didn't care a bit about either her or her family. Had she paused and looked at the whole situation through the eyes

of her (then future) brother-in-law, she would have seen
how her own family seemed so completely involved with
the intricacies of each other's lives that in fact pulling away
and beginning a separate life seemed like a perfectly reasonable response. The action wasn't objectionable, but
rather the style!

Finally, after many years, Margaret stopped trying to
make excuses for her husband and just enjoyed him as the
man she loved. If others in the family couldn't handle it,
that was their problem. (Although nobody had ever expressed aloud their objections to him, the nonverbal cues
and the lack of ease that permeated the room when everyone was together made it rather obvious.)

Years passed before Jennifer finally decided that she absolutely had to raise the subject with Margaret. They
talked, cried, negotiated, and finally decided to enjoy each
other as much as possible when Joel wasn't around, and to
fully reopen their communication channels. They found
that part of Jennifer's hostility toward Joel stemmed from
her feelings of being abandoned by her sister and closest
friend; and these feelings were exacerbated by the fact that
Margaret had chosen to marry a man who seemed to resist
letting her be a part of Jennifer's life. In fact, Margaret may
have chosen to marry someone so different from her own
family in order to build a life somewhat apart from the
strong enmeshment that had characterized her family. Jennifer also felt her sister's marriage had catapulted her out
into the world on her own—perhaps freer to travel and
live in other countries, but also vulnerable to the world
without her sibling support.

Like Jennifer, many women believe that they have no
right to express their feelings about their sister's prospec-
tive husband or lover, and that their comments would not

be welcomed anyway. Often, however, they are. But comments do not *have* to be critical and judgmental. They can merely be questions, inquisitive remarks aimed at helping the sister who is not getting married or involved understand *why* her sister treasures this particular person.

If either Jennifer or Margaret had attempted a more honest and open dialogue sooner, their relationship would have probably been more satisfying during the early years of Margaret's marriage. Jennifer would have been able to express whatever was on her mind in an open, respectful, inquisitive manner, and Margaret could have done the same. When sisters respond to each other in this fashion, the sister getting married has an opportunity to articulate her most positive perceptions about her future partner. Hearing the happiness and joy in Margaret's voice, Jennifer might have more readily accepted her brother-in-law.

Like many sisters, Jennifer and Margaret had different approaches to many aspects of life. Their tastes in men, styles, food, and recreation reflect their respective views of the world and how they function in it. The ability to accept these differences early on would have kept the lines of communication open during the first years of Margaret's marriage. We all want our sisters to realize that we have our own unique, basic needs and requirements, which can be brought out by husbands and lovers. Accepting them does not mean we are rejecting our sisters. Yet, because we grew up in the same room, shared the same eyeliner, and swooned over the same matinee idols, we somehow think that our needs are identical.

As are so many sisters who remain single after their sister marries, Jennifer was expected to look for someone like her sister's husband. ("Look at me. My life is good, I'm happy, we have a beautiful life.") Because Jennifer never expressed her negative impressions of Joel, her silence was taken as an acceptance of him and his "type." With more discussion, these two women could have realized how very different their goals, expectations, and needs really were. Sisters should be aware of the tendency to dismiss other's values and goals at all stages of their relationship.

But let's face facts. No matter how Jennifer had responded, Margaret would still have married Joel. They are very much in love, and their marriage serves them well. They have made a life for themselves that suits both their needs. However, by articulating the fact that she would not have chosen it, Jennifer is not indicting Margaret's life—she's just saying that it's not the life for her.

It took many years of distancing for both Margaret and Jennifer to feel comfortable with this observation. In the meantime, both of the sisters grew in ways unknown to each other and today, fifteen years later, they are faced with getting to know each other as adults. This is extremely difficult, especially when so many years have passed with little open, meaningful communication. But it is not impossible.

As exemplified by the case of Jennifer, Margaret, and Joel, the introduction of any outside factor into an existing system changes that system. Often I hear women express a desperate desire for their sisters relationship to remain unchanged after one or the other falls in love. This is an unrealistic expectation, sure to bring trouble from the outset. The system has changed. That's a fact. Therefore, the relationship must change, too. It doesn't necessarily have to become worse, but it does have to change. Resisting this change is bound to be worse than the change itself.

The essence of the relationship, then, does not have to be altered if (and only if) the participants are able to acknowledge what is happening within them as it occurs. One woman told me she would not risk making herself vulnerable by telling her sister that she was afraid of losing her when she and her husband moved two thousand miles away. Instead, she pretended it didn't bother her, and her sister wondered why her older sister adopted such a stoic mien in the face of this traumatic move. What, she asked, would it do to their phone calls and weekly luncheons? Until they eventually opened up to each other and tapped the source of their miscommunication, the younger sister believed her sibling wasn't disturbed by the fact that they would only be seeing each other once a year.

Communication—especially about such personal matters as the loves in one's life—generally has more of a chance if sisters set aside time for each other. It is possible, and usually advisable, to exclude the husbands from these special times.

At a sisters seminar in southern California, women in their forties, fifties, and sixties were particularly sensitive to the difficulties of maintaining a satisfying sisters relationship separate from the spousal one. Too often wives become confused about the role of their sisters in their marital lives, forgetting that their husbands and sisters don't have to do *everything* together, that their own lives with their sisters can be separate.

One woman who has four sisters, all of whom live in the same city, was agitated because their five husbands didn't like to be together as much as the sisters did. Some of the

best-laid social plans were disrupted because a few of the
husbands didn't care to socialize with the "whole group"
and didn't feel as close to their brothers-in-law as the
wives would have liked. At their social get-togethers, the
women would often congregate in one room, forcing their
spouses into a social situation when they all would have
preferred to be elsewhere. At other times, the husbands
would insist that the sisters stay with them, and the entire
group would then try to plan something that could be
considered "fun" for everyone. Invariably, either the activ-
ity, the time, or the mood clashed with at least one of the
ten in the party, and the events ended up being only
stressful—an atmosphere that wasn't exactly improved by
the sisters' frantic desire for their husbands to "relax and
have a good time." The situation deteriorated and eventually these family gatherings became rare events.

In an attempt to understand what was going on, the
sisters convened to discuss the situation. They agreed that
their purpose in all of this was simply to be with each
other as often as possible. The women didn't care what
they did—they were just as happy whether they were
chatting in one of their living rooms, walking through the
park, going shopping, or taking in an afternoon movie.
And they realized that their schedules were flexible
enough so they could plan such events for themselves
without having to impose on their husbands. Their solution? Each sister approached her husband and presented
him with an alternative plan that would allow her to meet
her sisters frequently without her husband. That was it!
The husbands felt much less pressure, and when family
events *were* planned (like holiday celebrations) they were
far more responsive.

After this plan was disclosed, Millie, the middle sister in

this fivesome, was concerned that her husband, Joe, might feel "left out." Actually, he was relieved to have the time to himself. In the past, he had thought it inappropriate to speak up, because he knew how much his sisters-in-law and those family get-togethers meant to his wife. But after the "new plan" was put into effect, both Millie and Joe felt as if both their needs had been met. When they returned from their respective outings, she filled him in on the family news, and this ten-minute "recap" was just enough.

Not all women behave in quite such an enlightened manner in such circumstances. Many prefer to believe that their relationship with their sisters can remain exactly as it always has been, even with the new men in their lives. Danielle and Denice are twins who roomed together, took classes together, joined the same sorority, and spent most of their free time with one another. In their junior year of college, they had their first major crisis. Denice married a man she had been dating for two years. Shortly thereafter, Denice became pregnant and found herself in a number of new roles, including wife and mother, while still continuing as a student. Danielle became an enraptured observer, watching her sister go through the many experiences they had so often fantasized about together in the past.

Denice said she needed Danielle's help with the baby; Danielle, however, found it a tremendous imposition to be asked to look after the infant, since it interfered with her own work. She began to resent both her nephew and her brother-in-law for setting up this situation.

In another set of twins, seventy years old, the two women had been the youngest offspring in a family of four daughters and were raised in a strict household. When, at the age of sixteen, Pauline (the older twin by six

minutes) announced her plans to marry, Sadie, the
younger twin, was horrified. She could not understand
why her sister would leave her for this man! It was beyond
her comprehension that either of them could want to live
with someone else. Hadn't they been everything to each
other? Hadn't they survived together, coping with strict
parents and unkind older sisters? Who was going to be her
"teammate" if her sister married?

This upset is not uncommon, particularly with twins,
and especially when one is ready for marriage and the
other isn't. Sadie was so upset by the marriage of her sister
that she wed within a few months, choosing a man who
was "the wrong match for me." She explains: "I had to
connect with someone because I couldn't stand the
thought of not having anybody in Pauline's place. I
thought a husband could replace her. I eventually tried
twice, but nobody could replace her. Nobody can serve the
role we serve for each other."

Today, in their older years, Pauline and Sadie live within
a short car ride from each other after having lived three
thousand miles apart for most of their adult lives. Sadie is
still married to her second husband, although he remains
insensitive to some of the intricacies of the sisters bond
into which he married. He does not appear to be
threatened by Pauline and Sadie's relationship, and as
long as they spend most of their time together, away from
home, he seems to think that he might as well accommodate the relationship since he cannot intercede anyway.
He did once say, however, that if his wife had to choose
between saving him and saving Pauline, he was confident
she would choose her twin. He claims that he doesn't
think about the implications of that very much.

Another aspect of the husbands and lovers issue is making yourself available to your sister if she needs to talk about whether she and the person she loves are well matched. Jennifer and Margaret, discussed earlier in this chapter, never had the opportunity to discuss their feelings about Margaret's choice. But fifty-eight-year-old Ellie, the second eldest of three girls and two boys, has remained estranged from one of her sisters because, according to Ellie, her sibling "went ahead and married this bloke when I told her he wasn't any good for her. He had no breeding, couldn't make a good living, and just isn't a pleasant guy to be around. I warned her, and now when she has marital problems, she expects me to be there for her. If she had listened to me in the first place, she would have avoided all this hassle and saved us all a lot of heartache. With him in the family, it was hard to relate to her because she always catered to him."

Although her intentions are good, her methods could use some improvement. Her judgmental attitude won't benefit either one of them, and if Ellie had been able to offer her opinion in a more supportive fashion, her sister might have been more willing to listen. In *On Becoming a Person*, Carl Rogers writes that the major barrier to interpersonal communication lies in our very natural tendency to judge—to approve or disapprove of the statements of others. Criticism is one of the most common methods of judging, and few of us know how to give constructive criticism well. We tend to accuse others and blithely offer our opinions without considering the person on the receiving end, seldom waiting until we are asked before expressing our views.

Admittedly, giving and receiving feedback about another individual is difficult for everyone. After all, criticizing your sister's spouse is tantamount to criticizing her life choices and values. It is far more helpful, and less destructive to the relationship, to deal with the issue of spouses as you would want it dealt with yourself. How would you want your sister to address this issue if you were in her place? What would be acceptable language? What would be unacceptable? Exactly why are you stating your views? Is there anything beneficial that can come out of this encounter? What is it? What do you want the end result to be? How can you most easily arrive at that result? How are you and your sister different in the ways you give and take criticism or opinions? How might you need to adjust what you were going to say to better accommodate your sister and her style?

Most of us will accept a solicited remark if it is offered with love, care, and respect for all parties involved. It is vital that you keep the criticism behavior oriented and be careful not to attack. As a parent feels protective of his/her child when the child is being attacked, so does a woman whose spouse is under fire: "What do you know anyway? Why are you telling me this? For my own good? Do you know my own good? Do you care to know what it is about me that I feel is valued when I am with this person? Do you know that he makes me feel something that I do not feel when I am in our family system? Wouldn't you like to know what that is? If you care to know, I'll tell you, and then I'll listen to your comments if you still feel they are valid."

Sisters who are still competing for the limelight as adults have a difficult time with dating and marriage. Their men become the object of comparison in their eyes. Still trying to outdo the other, they pursue their dates with a fervor of competition unmatched by that in any other arena. Their men become objects. What does he look like? What does he do? How much does he earn? The intrinsic worth of these attributes is not what is important here, but rather their relation to the sister's mate.

Mary and Diane, two sisters who live in Los Angeles, spend a lot of time together, both in their social and professional lives. Diane is a physical therapist and Mary, a teacher, helps out in her sister's office when one of the staff is on vacation. Mary has been divorced twice, and Diane has never been married, but had been courting a man for about five years and was about to be wed. Two months prior to Diane's wedding, however, Mary decided to announce her own impending (third) marriage to a man she had met only a short time before. She thought it would be a good idea for the sisters to get married within a week or two of each other and take their honeymoons together. But neither of the men liked each other especially well, and Diane wasn't excited by the idea.

Mary had a difficult time accepting her sister's wedding and the knowledge that she would now be "the single one." Nor did she like the idea of being out of the limelight while the family made a big deal about her sister's wedding. Ironically, it was Diane—who had been single for all her thirty-six years—who eventually postponed her wedding. Mary went through with hers.

These two women rejected the opportunity to examine their relationship and their style of communication, probably because both of them were getting something from their dynamic. Even though they agreed that their circumstances were unpleasant, apparently it was not uncomfortable enough for either to initiate a change. Their patterns served them well; each gained something from seeing herself as the innocent victim of the other. Whenever possible, each would engage someone in a discussion about what the other had just done, going into great detail about the manipulative tactics involved. But neither would dare share her perceptions with her sister, feeling more comfortable discussing them with others, always ending any story with such questions as, "Is this any way for a sister to act?" "Why isn't she happy for me and my happiness?"

In order to break down barriers and establish constructive feedback about spouses or lovers, the following suggestions may be helpful. They are based on communication principles from assertiveness training, interpersonal relations, and conflict management.

Try to be descriptive rather than judgmental in your appraisal. Your comments will probably be received more openly. Rochelle, for instance, was hesitant about talking to her sister Martha about her concern over her brother-in-law's frequent business trips. However, she was deeply troubled that Martha had to stay alone for two weeks at a time when he was away. She found herself becoming angry at Jack for leaving Martha alone so much of the time. Whenever they were together, she would never miss an opportunity to remind Jack of how lonely it must be for Martha, and she would ask whether he really had to be away from home so often.

Rochelle would sometimes raise this topic with her sister, and when she did, Martha would quickly dismiss it, saying that it didn't bother her, and that Jack's business required him to travel extensively. But in truth, she didn't want Rochelle to come down heavily on her husband because she didn't want to share with her sister the fact that she hated to be alone while he was away.

Once Rochelle became convinced that she was sincerely concerned for Martha and that her anger at Jack may have been misplaced, she asked Martha if they could talk. "I'm terribly concerned about you staying alone so much of the time when Jack's out of town, and I find myself getting angry at him and wanting to make him feel guilty for leaving you," she told her sister. "I don't want to keep disturbing you and him about this, but that's what's behind all my carping. I see I was wrong in getting angry at him, but I want you to know that I worry about you and wish we could do something about the amount of time you are alone each month."

Martha appreciated the manner in which Rochelle approached the topic—nonjudgmentally, specifically, and taking the responsibility for her own actions. She finally admitted to being concerned about being alone so much, but said she didn't want to complain about the situation since Jack's job offered them so many benefits.

Touched by her sister's concern, Martha decided to spend more time with Rochelle and the rest of the family when Jack was out of town. Rochelle had a guest room where Martha could stay whenever Jack was away.

Another communication suggestion is to steer away from labels. Most sisters grow up under the shroud of one label or another (see Chapter 3), so to hear a sister label from someone else only perpetuates an unwelcome pattern.

Being specific is more effective than generalizing. A word of caution, however: the potential problem with specificity is that it often makes the criticism sound too much like an attack. Avoid terms such as "they say" or "most people." Use instead "it seems to me" or "the way I see it." If the point is worth making, then it is important enough to be specific in your own mind about how you feel about it. Assume responsibility for the statement and be able to back it up with particular examples of exactly what you would like to see done differently. Remember that the best intentions can be offset by a barrage of attacks. Be clear about what is disturbing you as a caring, loving sister.

Also, make a point of speaking only for yourself. Sisters feel attacked if they sense they were the subject of a family caucus that resulted in a collective recommendation being passed on through you. Repeat the important "I feel" or "it seems to me" or "I think" in order to make the feedback more personal and direct. Don't worry about sounding apologetic. If indeed you believe it may be none of your business, but what you see bothers you anyway, then say so! Sitting by docilely and watching something that makes you feel uncomfortable without saying anything doesn't mean your message isn't being conveyed through nonverbal means.

CHAPTER 7

ASSESSING YOUR RELATIONSHIP WITH YOUR SISTER

"I'm trying to find a way to say or do something that will help my sister feel less competitive with me."

Women frequently tell me, "I wish my sister were . . ." I invite you now to confront what you would be willing to accept relative to change in yourself, your sister, and your relationship. Often we tend to romanticize the sibling connection and have extremely unrealistic expectations of what we can and cannot get from it. Change, at best, even with willing parties, is usually a slow, incremental process.

In the seminars and in my work with families, women have told me that the following questions have provided them with increased insight into their sisters relationship. I encourage you to respond as honestly as you can; the value of these questions depends on the truthfulness with which you respond. There are no right or wrong replies, but before examining where you would like you and your sister to be, I advise you to first examine where you are now. Try to make an objective assessment of your relationship. When you know where you are now, and you have decided where you would like to be, then you can best determine the appropriate way to get there.

This exercise is designed to assist you in focusing on those specific areas in which you experience the most difficulty getting along with your sibling. Ultimately, this awareness of your communication style will enable you to broaden and strengthen your sister bond.

Overall Relationship with Sister

Do you have a satisfying relationship with your sister, and do you feel she really knows you?

Do you and your sister have an equal bond, or does one of you assume a leadership role?

Are you threatened by your sister's accomplishments, and do they interfere with your relationship? Are you threatened by her failures? Do they interfere?

Expression of Emotions

Are feelings generally discussed, or are they avoided altogether?

Do you feel comfortable openly expressing feelings of affection and praise? Is your sister able to communicate these same feelings?

Perceptions of Roles

Have you and your sister continued childhood roles into adulthood? Are these roles flexible or rigid, and are they based on the needs of situations?

Have there been changes in the roles that you and your sister assume regarding your parents? If so, how have they changed and in what direction?

Has your perception of your sister changed over time?

Encouragement of Growth

Are you likely to encourage your sister's involvement in new activities or interests, whether or not you share those interests?

Does your sister support you in personal growth efforts?

As time goes on, do you see your relationship with your sister maturing? If so, how? If not, does it bother you that the relationship has remained fundamentally the same?

Self-evaluation

Do you find that you compare yourself with your sister?

Do you find that your opinion of yourself is influenced by your sister's opinion of you?

Do you find that you compete with your sister in areas of social, professional, or family life?

Interaction with Sister

How often do you spend time with your sister alone, in groups, and in family settings?

When you and your sister disagree, do you find that issues from your childhood interfere with resolving the current problem?

Do you seek your sister's counsel when you have a problem? Does this counsel, in general, tend to be judgmental or supportive?

Other Family Members

What effect do other family members (parents, spouses, children) have on your relationship?

In what ways do your parents or children either inhibit or encourage a close bond with your sister?

Do you and your sister relate differently to each other when spouses or lovers are present?

Personal Issues

Do you have difficulty forgiving your sister for something that happened in the past?

If you really shared your true feelings or perceptions with your sister, do you fear that it might jeopardize your relationship?

How has geographical distance or closeness affected your relationship?

Conflict/Resolution

When a point of conflict arises between you and your sister, do the two of you tend to attempt to address it or do you usually avoid it?

When you have a conflict, are the two of you usually capable of resolving it yourselves? If not, do you invite other people or do other people volunteer to mediate in your disagreements and, if so, who and under what circumstances?

Which of you is more likely to compromise or let go of the problem?

Miscellaneous

If your relationship is successful, what makes it so?

If you recall a time in the past when you and your sister were on better terms than you are now, what has contributed to the change?

If your relationship with your sister is better now than it was in the past, what has changed to make this possible?

What have you learned from your sister?

What positive qualities about yourself do you attribute to having been a sister to————? *(fill in with sister's name)*

What do you see as the basis for any rivalry existing today?

Do you perceive your sister as intruding into your special friendships with other women?

What do you like and admire about your sister?

What does your sister like and admire about you?

How would you like to see your relationship change?

How do you contribute to the aspects of your relationship that you find unpleasant and annoying?

How does your sister contribute to the aspects of your relationship that you consider unpleasant and annoying?

Imagine this fantasy: you and your sister are as happy as you could be. How old would you be? Where would you be? What other characteristics of the fantasy can you pinpoint?

How would you like to raise your daughters to be like you and your sister?

What are the most positive aspects of your relationship?

Describe your sister as she would describe herself.

Describe yourself as your sister would describe you.

How would your sister describe your relationship?

How has your relationship evolved over the last ten years?

In what ways do you feel closer to your sister now than you did ten years ago? Twenty years ago? Thirty years ago? What, if anything, has changed as those years have passed?

If you knew that either you or your sister had only one more week to live, what would you most want to tell or ask her?

Of these questions, you may have preferred to pick and choose those that seemed most relevant. Take note if you have avoided questions because they have been either too difficult or too emotionally charged to answer comfortably. In the following chapter, these areas will be explored in greater depth.

CHAPTER 8

STARTING DOWN THE PATH TOWARD BETTER COMMUNICATION

"Sometimes I say things to my sister that make me sound so critical and I often think, 'Does she know how much I really love and enjoy her?'"

Now that you have a better sense of your expectations for your relationship, it's time to examine more closely exactly how you and your sister communicate. In this chapter, I will use various scenarios to illustrate the skills that can be useful in helping you and your sister communicate more effectively. But remember: even if all of the techniques are familiar to you, breaking ingrained communication patterns will not be easy. It will take time, effort, and commitment.

The process toward improved communication requires, too, that you assume responsibility for what happens between you and your sibling. Be honest. You must consider, as objectively as possible, the consequences of change. And how committed are you, really? What are you willing to do in order to facilitate an improved relationship between the two of you? What are you willing to disclose?

Are you willing to modify your behavior with your sister? Are you willing to try new skills with your sister?

If your relationship with your sister has not been based on trust, or has had some major gaps regarding the quality of communication, I suggest that when you try some of the suggestions in this chapter, you do so methodically. And even if they don't work initially, don't give up; try again in a few weeks. Expanding or rebuilding trust takes tremendous effort. Although it may be tempting at times to throw up your hands and say, "Well, I tried, and she's not interested! How am I supposed to do it alone?" there *is* usually an answer, and it may be more easily discernible if you allow yourself some time to reflect.

Special rules and guidelines must frequently be incorporated into a sisterly relationship for it to function well. Certain situations may seem unresolvable, as when one sister reacts adversely to her brother-in-law's demanding behavior. In such cases, if these women cannot resolve the matter between themselves, it should be set aside and considered "not discussable," so that it doesn't interfere with *their* relationship. With such issues out of the way, other tools of communication (asking for what you want, phrasing requests and comments kindly, handling a sibling's verbal attack, and giving advice without sounding judgmental) can be managed more effectively.

In this chapter I will introduce you to communication exercises that will help you examine various situations more insightfully, so that you can stop responding to circumstances in unsatisfying and unproductive ways. Once you begin practicing these exercises on your own and with your sister, you will gradually see a profound change in the way you and your sister relate.

For most of us, our communication styles are based primarily on what we observed about the way our parents communicated. And our parents developed their communication style based on what they observed between *their* parents. Regardless of whether or not this model was ideal, sisters tend to incorporate the way they were spoken to as children into their communication style as adults.

Eileen, forty-five, and Nicole, forty-two, learned from their parents that it was wrong to express their negative feelings. They were consistently rewarded for showing only their positive feelings. If something happened that upset them, they were told, "Cheer up. Don't make such a big deal. Smile and it will feel better."

When Eileen was grounded because of her messy room, she threw a tantrum and was punished for it. "What else was I supposed to do?" she recalled. "Looking back, the only feelings Mom or Dad had ever shown were their angry ones, and I guess they were so scared of them that they didn't want us ever to be angry. How unrealistic! When I think of it, I realize they never showed any other kind of feeling, either. Whenever Mom or Dad got upset, they yelled at each other, threw things, and ranted and raved. Yet when I did it, I was reprimanded. As children we weren't allowed to get angry."

Given the message—implicitly and explicitly—that expressing anger was unacceptable, Eileen and Nicole all too often let their angry feelings go unaddressed. And, unfortunately, their parents failed to provide them with alternative behaviors or responses.

As adults, Eileen and Nicole's interactions were typified by putdowns and sarcasm. Eileen told me, "My folks expressed their endearment by being caustic and sarcastic. As a child, this felt lousy; in fact, as an adult it *still* feels lousy. Yet, my sister and I now relate to each other in this manner, even though neither of us likes it. It seems to be the way we were trained, and even though we know how damaging it is, neither of us has the skills to stop perpetuating the cycle."

Very often sisters assume: "We were raised in the same household, we should be the same." This is a fallacy. In reality, each girl/woman internalizes the parental mode of communication and makes it her own—tempered by *her* experiences, *her* friends, *her* personality, and so forth. And though women like Eileen and Nicole have learned, smiling through clenched teeth, to pretend that everything is okay, these patterns *can* and must be changed. "Unlearning" a destructive dynamic is as important as learning a constructive one, and there are many areas to be addressed. But, first, let's address the problem behind the complaint I hear from so many sisters: "She doesn't listen to me." *Listening* is our first area of improvement.

Listening is much more than hearing. It is a complex, multifaceted process characterized by understanding what the other person is actually saying. Many factors play a role in your ability to listen, among them your own perceptual filters, your environment, verbal and nonverbal cues, that relationship you have with your sister, your willingness to follow what she is saying with body *and* mind, and the larger context of the communication.

Few of us are good listeners. Before you take offense, think about it. You may very well pay attention in order to get the gist of what is being said—but are you *really* addressing the core of what she is saying? Do you demonstrate the skills of an attentive listener through your body position, gestures, eye contact, and responses? Each of us is acutely aware of the impact of another's nonverbal communication upon us, but are we as inclined to consider the impact upon others of *our* own nonverbal messages?

Elizabeth, fifty-four, and Alexandra, forty-nine, were discussing Elizabeth's upcoming voyage to Europe. This was to be her first journey alone, and she was anxious about the prospect of staying in hotels and eating in restaurants unaccompanied. Alexandra tried to bolster her confidence. "Nonsense! You'll do just fine! Think of all those exciting places! I'll give you a list of places to see, markets to shop at, restaurants with exotic foods, and you'll have a ball."

Alexandra's response was more like that of a travel agent than a sister. So Elizabeth tried again to convey her trepidation, this time requesting specific suggestions to help her overcome her nervousness. Again, Alexandra dismissed her feelings by addressing how busy she would be and all the spectacular places she would see, moralizing along the way with several "shoulds" ("you ought to" or "shouldn't do that"). In the process, Alexander diverted their attention from the crux of the problem, and consequently Elizabeth decided to drop it. Alexandra decided that her sister simply wasn't willing to take her well-traveled and experienced advice.

It was not all Alexandra's fault. Elizabeth should have clearly restated to her sister exactly *how* she felt—not only about the upcoming trip, but also about what she perceived to be Alexandra's dismissive response. She could have said, "Alexandra, I am frightened of being alone on this trip. When you say, 'Nonsense!' it makes me feel as if you think I am a child, and I feel silly. I know that traveling alone is not a problem for you, but I have never done it before and I am feeling nervous. It would be helpful to me if you could understand this from my point of view." And she might have further added, "What are some concrete suggestions you can offer about preventing these feelings of loneliness and fear? What shall I do if I feel overwhelmed?"

Had she presented her needs in this forthright, sensitive manner, Elizabeth would have defined her insecurities much more explicitly, and her request for Alexandra's help would have created a nondefensive, open atmosphere. Unless Alexandra is made to genuinely understand the impact of this trip on her sister, how can she possibly empathize?

In the future, when Elizabeth shares her feelings with her sister, she must make sure that Alexandra does not feel accused of being a "bad listener" or an "insensitive person." Rather, she should be made to feel positive about her attempts to understand Elizabeth's perspective—otherwise, she may fail to be receptive for fear of encountering a negative response.

Other aspects of listening also found lacking among sisters include those that center around the physical manifestations of our attentiveness. Do you listen with your whole body? Do your eyes wander? Do you look away when someone walks by? Do you face each other? Are your arms folded across your chest, possibly giving the impression that you're not open to what is being said? Communication is an interactive process, and beyond your verbal responses, you must be vigilantly aware of your nonverbal signals. When your sister is talking, *you* are communicating your level of interest in, commitment to, and patience with what she is saying.

Do you listen to each other in a comfortable setting or are there other distractions and interruptions? If the site is not conducive to conversation, suggest that the two of you visit in a quiet, neutral setting—you can go for a walk, sit in a coffee shop, or even in the car—away from phones and other distractions. Try to reserve quality, uninterrupted time to devote to each other.

All of us have occasionally let our thoughts interfere with what someone is saying. When that happens with your sister, interrupt her and ask her to repeat what she just said. Admitting that you didn't hear something is much more acceptable and appreciated than pretending to follow.

Consider the positive interactions between two sisters, Dawn and Arlene. As Dawn, fifty-eight, was leaving work one evening, she overheard a co-worker make a deprecatory comment about her age in relation to her efficiency on the job. She had planned to meet her sister Arlene, fifty-one, for a short visit after work, but, stunned and depressed by this comment, she wasn't sure now that she was ready to talk to anyone about this. When Dawn arrived, Arlene sensed instantly that something was wrong, but instead of blurting out, "You look awful! Did you lose your best friend or did the roof cave in? Come on, tell me," she waited to see if Dawn would be forthcoming with whatever was troubling her. When, after a few minutes, it became apparent that this wouldn't happen, Arlene said gently, "You look like something is bothering you. Care to talk about it?" Then, instead of jumping in and prodding more—"Tell me, tell me"—she simply looked at her sister and waited.

Haltingly, Dawn started to talk about what had happened. Instead of saying, "Oh, it can't be that bad," Arlene responded with, "It seems pretty hard to talk about. Take your time. We have lots of it." Once Arlene had heard the full story, she reacted not only to what had been said but to how the comment seemed to have affected her sister: "It sounds as if you weren't only hurt by the reference to your age, but also that you are having doubts about job security. It seems only yesterday that we were in high school together, and now we are overhearing comments about age."

As Dawn continued, Arlene sat attentively, demonstrating her interest by looking at her, interjecting with, "Yes . . . . Go on . . . Really? . . . For instance? . . . I understand," and interrupting occasionally to paraphrase what she understood Dawn to say. Throughout the conversation she kept in mind that if her sister was hearing comments about her age, she too would soon be hearing similar comments. This helped her empathize with Dawn.

Unlike Alexandra in the earlier example, Arlene made a genuine effort to show her sister she was impressed not only with what her sister was saying, but also with the feelings accompanying her statements. Through her comments and actions, Arlene allowed Dawn to continue without interrupting, offering encouragement along the way. She avoided making value judgments, or telling her what she "should" do. Nor did she offer advice. Rather, as the conversation progressed, she helped Dawn decide what, if anything, she wanted to do, and by letting her sister talk it out, she could hear and then "play back" Dawn's own suggestions by rephrasing them whenever necessary.

This kind of "reflective listening" is discussed at length by noted psychologist Dr. Carl Rogers in two of his books, *Client-centered Therapy* and *On Becoming a Person.* By restating the feelings and content of what your sister has communicated, you demonstrate not only understanding, but also your acceptance of her. Arlene's paraphrasing of what she thought Dawn had said clarified it for her and enabled Dawn to feel there was someone who was sincerely interested in *her*—and willing to listen.

Keep in mind that words mean different things to different people; your understanding of a particular word or phrase may be quite different from your sister's, and thus much can be gained by clarifying.

Of course, many things could have gone differently for Dawn and Arlene. What if Dawn had chosen *not* to tell her sister what was on her mind? In an accepting sisters relationship, this is an option that is allowable and sometimes even encouraged. It is essential that you be able to maintain your own private thoughts when you feel the need to, without concern that your sister will feel excluded or threatened, and with the assurance that she will respect your privacy. However, because sisters have shared so much through the years, they may have a hard time with this notion. Try to remember that no matter how close you are to your sister, she is bound to need her private time.

If Dawn had been uncomfortable revealing what was on her mind, Arlene *could* have prodded, "Oh, come on, I can read you like a book and I know something is bothering you. You'll feel better if you tell me." Or, "I tell you everything; come on, don't ruin our evening by being such a sourpuss." Or, "Are you feeling like talking yet?"

A more empathic response would have let Dawn keep her thoughts to herself, while acknowledging her apparent displeasure. In such a situation, it is valuable to leave the communication door open, however, by saying, "I can see you don't want to talk about it now. Sometimes it's useful to just have some time to think. I hope you work it out. If you want to talk about it another time, or if I can help you in any way, please let me know." Then ask what your sister would like to talk about or do *right now*. She may want to be distracted for a while. If so, leave the primary issue alone.

For healthy, open communication, then, sisters must become sensitive to each other's emotional state. After a scenario like the one described above, you could call and "check in" a day or two later, saying, "I was thinking of you, and I hope that whatever was disturbing you the other evening is in the process of being resolved." Or, "You are in my thoughts, and I just wanted you to know that." By being undemanding and accepting, your sister will be able to sense your caring and not perceive your actions as intrusive.

My seminars have convinced me that many women need to improve their capacity to respond to the "feeling cues" their sisters send them. Ask yourself, "How would I feel if I were experiencing what she is going through?" But be careful; it's useful not only to think of how *you* would feel, but also to put yourself in your sister's position, imagining how *she* may feel.

This exercise is not a magical solution. You may end up being right on target—or way off base. Don't presume you *know* how she feels, but only that you have an idea about how she feels. There's a difference. "I know just how you feel" is a far less empathic response than, "You seem to be disturbed." When the communication between the two of you is open in this fashion, it's easier to validate specific feelings by deciding whether or not your descriptions are accurate.

Focus on the nuances of the exchange with your sister before you respond to what she is saying. Make every attempt to let her finish her thought. Avoid sitting on the edge of your chair, shaking your head back and forth frantically, waiting for the moment to interrupt so that you can present your reply. In fact, *don't even think of formulating your reply until she has finished.* This is especially difficult for sisters who often pride themselves on knowing what the other is thinking. Too often, a few moments after she begins to make her point, the sister who is listening is already responding in her own head. But in formulating her reply before "her turn," she is bound to have difficulty giving her undivided attention. If you and your sister are going to develop interactions that are respectful of and responsive to one another—ones in which you both are confident that the other is making a concerted effort to hear what is being said—you both *must* learn to listen.

Let's assume you are willing to work hard to enhance your communication with your sister. I want you to consider three areas essential for effective communication already mentioned in Chapter 4 of this book and described by Dr. Robert Bolton in *People Skills.* They are: genuineness, nonpossessive love, and empathy. Let me review them again below.

Some women complain that "my sister doesn't know me." How could she, if you are not presenting your true self? You need to take the responsibility to present who you really are to your sister. If you're always feeling as if you should be on your "best behavior" when you're together, tell her you feel as though you are being scrutinized and how uncomfortable that is for you. Tell her you want her to get to know you as you really are. It is imperative that you be honest—about your feelings, desires, and requirements of one another—and that you maintain enough flexibility to meet the changing demands of any given situation.

It's not that easy. Being at peace with yourself is the key to being willing to share yourself with your sister. It is only through increased self-awareness and *your* acceptance of who you are, that you will feel freer to express your true self. If you apply this process to all the relationships in your life, you'll find that your ability to accept yourself—with all your attributes and frailties—will help you accept others and, in turn, make them more accepting of *you*.

Dr. Carl Rogers describes the second aspect—nonpossessive love—as loving a person as she is. He is not referring to the possessive, romantic connotations of the word *love*. Instead, he is referring to the type of love theologians call *agape*, which entails an *unselfish* concern for the well-being of your sister. You don't have to like her—in fact, there will probably be many aspects of her that are quite "unlikable." But sisters can express love and acceptance for one another without liking everything about each other. In this manner, they are free to express their opinions of one another nonjudgmentally.

The third component—empathy—has already been touched on earlier in this chapter. Empathy requires that you not only understand how your sister thinks about a specific situation, but that you also feel what she might be feeling. In her work with adults and children, Dr. Norma Feshbach, a psychologist at the University of California at Los Angeles, has described a three-part model of empathy, in which a person is not only able to perceive a given situation, but is also able to project herself into that situation, and, finally, is able to feel the emotion the person having the experience is feeling.

It *is* possible to identify with your sister's perceptions and feelings. On the dust jacket of this book is a figure-ground perception test. (The *figure* is the part of the image that stands out for you against the *ground*.) If, when you and your sister looked at the cover, you perceived the women's faces first, but your sister perceived the vase first, you have different perceptions. You look at the same image but see different things. "Don't you see it? It's so clear," you may say. But is it clear? Is it so easy to see what another person sees? Of course it isn't. And this is just a perception exercise; there's no emotion involved, no investment, no insistence to "see it my way." When some women examine their lives, they find that when there *is* an emotional investment, when it *is* important for one sister to have the other see her point, this is often the time when the unconvinced sister seems to remain the most steadfast.

In the weeks ahead, try relinquishing your point of view and looking at the world as best you can through your sister's eyes. My research, through seminars and interviews, has convinced me that this is what your sister wants from you. And isn't it also what you want from her? Be honest with yourself. And with her.

Keep these factors in mind as we move into another major area of concern among sisters—namely, the manner in which we offer criticism to each other.

Effective criticism is directed at a situation or a condition; it is *not* directed at a person. However, a common complaint from many women is that they feel their sister is criticizing their essence, their personality, or their character attributes. (Perhaps this is a reversion to juvenile exchanges from many years earlier, which contained messages that might have been age-appropriate then, but are certainly not now.)

Critical comments are more likely to be accepted if they are targeted to a particular situation. We all have so many dimensions—when you feel attacked as a whole person, it's natural to feel defensive. At the same time, it may seem as though your sister perceives you as a one-dimensional being, incapable of having different responses.

But sisters who offer each other *constructive* criticism usually avoid attacking personality traits, with the result being that the sister on the receiving end isn't made to feel as if her entire self-image is on the line. These siblings are careful to address the specific issue at hand, avoiding labels or historical references such as, "You always do that. When will you ever learn?" If a sister attacks or feels attacked, she may be less likely to listen to the content of the criticism because so much of her energy is being poured into protecting her vulnerable side. Derisive comments and destructive criticism can create hostility, and rarely bring about the kind of behavior we would like to see either in ourselves or our sisters. Don't let yourself learn this the hard way.

One day, Jennie, twenty-four, decided that she was fed up with her sister, Millie, twenty-two, for repeatedly borrowing her jewelry without asking. She considered hurling degrading insults at Millie when she returned home to their apartment, but then she reconsidered. Maybe she shouldn't say anything at all: "It wasn't such a big deal; I shouldn't be so attached to material things." Finally she decided she had a right to know when and if her sister was going to borrow her things. She didn't want to insult Millie, so she decided to approach her sister calmly and sensibly in a nonaccusatory fashion.

When Millie came home from work, Jennie fixed her a drink. As they sat in their living room, she said, "I would like you to ask me when you want to borrow my jewelry, so I'll know where it is. I'll probably loan it to you, but I would appreciate your asking me beforehand." At first, Millie was a little defensive; but then she admitted that Jennie had a every right to worry that the necklace might have been misplaced. She agreed to ask permission next time. She also thanked Jennie for not accusing her of stealing and for talking with her so calmly. They both were surprised by how simple the interaction had been, and the ease with which they handled—rather than avoided—a potential conflict.

Let's look at this same scenario, had Millie reacted quite differently. What if she had responded, "Are you implying that I am a thief? You're calling me irresponsible and I resent that! Anyway, what are you making such a big deal about? It's a dumb old beaded necklace, not a set of diamond earrings!"

Jennie could have responded, "You're a spoiled brat and I can't ever talk to you. I am not calling you a thief, but I *am* calling you inconsiderate." Or, "What I said seems to have made you angry. I didn't intend to make it a big issue, and I wasn't implying you were a thief. I *am* requesting that when you want to borrow my jewelry, you ask me. That way, I can know where it is and won't have to worry that it was either misplaced or stolen."

Until now Jennie's style had been either to avoid issues or become aggressive. When she did explode, her accusations included not only the issue at hand, but also a laundry list of all the times in the past when her sister had been inconsiderate, selfish, and spoiled.

Thank about the last time you and your sister were in a conflict. What happened? How did you feel? Was it dealt with the way you normally handle disagreements? Do you usually resolve issues together? Do others join in, or are they recruited to help? Do you often leave issues unresolved, never dealing with them again? Do either of you expect particular problems to be "solved" quickly? Whether or not the two of you are satisfied with your conflict-resolution pattern, it could be helpful for you to examine your style of conflict with your sister.

Sometimes our conflict styles change, depending on the situation in which we find ourselves. Something you say or do may inspire a particular reaction in your sister and then, in turn, she may say or do something. That's the way many disagreements escalate. But when properly managed, conflict need not be destructive. It may actually be *con*structive—renewing a relationship, or enabling people to move ahead in difficult family situations.

Organizational psychologists Drs. Kenneth Thomas and Ralph Kilmann designed a conflict-mode instrument based on the idea that every style consists of two partially competing goals—concern for self and concern for the other. According to these researchers, your styles may be competitive, collaborative, compromising, avoiding, or accommodating. None of these styles is inherently "bad." In fact, different situations require different styles. How sisters feel about their relationship can be seen in the level of concern each sister shows for the other's feelings, point of view, and creativity in finding a solution.

Too many sisters, of course, feel they haven't ever had a fight and their relationship is fine. But is this the result of good communication or simply a denial of differences? "Nothing is important enough to make an issue over," they often say. The fact that they may be harboring unvoiced resentments and jealousies doesn't enter into their perspective of whether or not their pattern of interacting is potentially destructive.

On the other hand, some sisters fight with each other constantly—believing, in fact, that their openly abusive expression of hostile feelings is proof that they care about each other. "If we didn't care, we wouldn't fight." But perhaps they are missing the point. If they really cared, wouldn't this dilute the venom of their confrontations?

If you and your sister are stuck in a conflict style that seems destructive and counterproductive, it's time for you to reexamine your rituals. Through empathic and reflective listening, stating your needs specifically and assertively, becoming more accepting of your sister, many of the destructive elements of conflicts can be avoided.

In order to control the level of conflict, you must resolve it while it's smoldering—and before it's in flames. By denying or avoiding the problem, you may be cheating yourself, your sister, and your relationship.

As you work on your relationship with your sister, try to understand *why* you act a particular way. If your own style is "competitive," this can be manifested in behavior that is aggressive and uncooperative. Maybe you don't really care what her needs are; maybe you're primarily interested in getting your own needs met, at any cost. But even if a sarcastic, critical style works for you, is it the style you really want to perpetuate?

According to Drs. Kenneth Thomas and Ralph Kilmann, "accommodation" is another style of communication. Accommodating women place their sister's concerns above their own, projecting a cooperative but unassertive image. Usually there is an element of self-sacrifice to this attitude, which may take the form of charity—yielding to another's point of view or taking an order even when they'd rather not. These women mention feeling that their ideas or concerns are not getting the attention they deserve, that they have little influence in the relationship, that their needs are not recognized, and that their sisters do not respect them.

When you realize you are wrong, acknowledging alternative solutions shows that you are reasonable. So, when something is more important to your sister than it is to you, try to be accommodating.

Another style employed by women who were taught not to make a big deal about anything is "avoidance." Sisters who are avoiders can be characterized as both unassertive and uncooperative. As mentioned earlier, conflicts between these women are not addressed because they diplomatically talk around an issue, put it off to another time, or pull back from a potentially uncomfortable situation. These women don't pursue their own goals, nor do they pursue their sister's concerns. They rarely offer their own ideas, so their sister never knows their thoughts. Often they are so careful to avoid any confrontation that others around them feel uncomfortable. Any decisions these women make are usually made by default, and they tend to feel overwhelmed by the prospect of doing any family business simply because the thought of raising any issues with their siblings is so frightening.

But, like the others, the avoiding style does serve its purpose—when, for example, an issue is trivial, or when there is no chance of satisfying one's own needs, or when the potential damage of a confrontation outweighs the benefits of its resolution, or when more information is needed before arriving at a conclusion.

Some women choose a "collaborative" style, in which they are both assertive about their own needs and cooperative with their sister. This way the women deal only with the situation, but collaborate in trying to find a solution respectful of their own and their sister's needs. These women attempt to find the source of the problems so they can arrive at a creative, insightful solution that meets both of their needs. In these cases, the solution is usually one that neither sister had initially envisioned, but rather had discovered together after sifting through both sets of concerns.

This style can be extremely useful when each sister feels that her own concerns are too important to be compromised, when sisters want to learn more about each other, or when it would be useful to merge insights. Since collaboration takes considerable time and energy, women typically find themselves discussing their conflicts at length. But some issues need a quicker solution, so you can end up wasting a lot of time and energy. It can also be disappointing to put so much into solving problems with someone who isn't also willing to do so. If this is your predominant style and your sister does not want to participate, it may be because of some conflicting interests, defensiveness, or impatience.

The last style discussed by Thomas and Kilmann is the "compromising" style, which falls between assertiveness and cooperativeness. Women who employ this style probably want to find a solution quickly, one that both they and their sister will find acceptable and partially satisfying. Some women feel this is an appropriate style when their goals are moderately important, but not worth the effort of being more assertive. Some sisters might choose this mode to temporarily settle a larger, more complex issue. Compromising is also a back-up pattern when other styles, such as collaboration or competition, are unsuccessful.

Every one of us has the capacity to use all of these five conflict-handling modes, although we each certainly have style preferences and no one uses just one style all of the time with her sister.

But no matter what your style, a satisfying relationship should always incorporate one sister's respect for the other. Particularly during a disagreement, one woman's lack of respect for her sibling may be telling that sister that she isn't respected as a person. If, in an argument, your sister treats you disrespectfully—calling you names and throwing all sorts of uncomfortable information at you—and then she apologizes afterward, you may wonder if she *really* meant what she said.

Keep in mind that words aren't the only vehicles for disrespectful thoughts; anger or suspicion can be conveyed through the simplest of gestures: the shift of a glance, the folding of one's arms.

I'd like to take a moment to reiterate the importance of understanding your sister's perspective and relaying your thoughts and feelings in a sensitive, helpful manner. Try to echo her content and feelings—from *her* point of view.

Only after your sister feels confident that you have heard and understood her should you then speak to her and express your perspective. When you finally do so, be clear about your perspective on the issue.

When you do get a chance to express your own thoughts, state them *briefly*. Stay away from degrading or disrespectful words. Calling your sister a dope, irresponsible, or insensitive won't exactly enhance your chances of her hearing and accepting what you have to say. Be aware that it is essential to disclose how you feel about a particular idea, topic, solution, or incident. If you feel accused or insulted by what your sister has said to you, tell her. The emotional issues have to be resolved before you can resolve the problems themselves.

If you are clear on what you want from your sister, you will be better able to ask her in a way that is specific, direct, and honest, violating neither her rights nor yours. By focusing on behavior, it won't seem as though you are *attacking* her. Ask for what you want using concise, direct statements, assuming responsibility for your requests. Make your request at a time that is comfortable for both of you, when you are alone, and watch your body language: look directly at her, speak in a fluent speech pattern and in normal volume. When you adhere to these guidelines, her response will more likely be the type of response you would like. In addition, don't forget the importance of telling your sister (also in terms of her behavior) what you like and appreciate about her. Saying something like, "You're always so thoughtful," isn't nearly as effective as, "Your thoughtfulness came shining through when you selected a card with a camel on it; I'll add it to my collection!"

In the years ahead, as you and your sister work to

strengthen your bond, keep in mind that the relationship is bound to change—just as the two of you change. What was important when you were both single may not be important when you are married or parents. Remain open to a flexibility of roles, especially in relation to aging or infirm parents, or to crises that may occur.

The beauty of the sisters relationship lies in the breadth of experience it offers. As the years pass, this person— who at one time may have known you well—can grow in relation to you. If you have been apart for years, it is still possible to reconnect. In my experience with sisters— whether they have been together for a lifetime, or have been separated for long periods by geographical or psychological distance—new and enriching patterns of communication and relating can be established as their lives unfold.

CHAPTER 9

SISTERS BY CHOICE

"We're soulmates. Our roles change all of the time,
and so comfortably—mother, sister, friend; age has
nothing to do with it."

Whether you are pleased or dissatisfied with your sisters
relationship—or even if you have no biological sister at
all—there is another viable, enriching female relationship
that millions of women have taken advantage of, namely a
"sisters-by-choice" relationship with a woman to whom
you are not biologically related. This bond may not necessarily fill a void in your own sisters relationship, but it can
provide you with a supportive, meaningful emotional connection.

Unlike biological sisters, women who are sisters by
choice have sought one another out. They may have different backgrounds, or come from different age brackets,

but they share a certain sense of themselves and of the world. They open doors that let their relationship grow while they each go through their normal life changes. Many women consider their sisters by choice to be more supportive, nonjudgmental, and honest than their biological siblings. Even so, one of the most encouraging aspects of these sisterlike relationships is that, as they mature, women can apply much of what they have learned from them to strengthen their unions with their biological sisters.

Tina and Darlene are sisters by choice who have known each other since their childhoods in New Jersey, and whose bond became quite strong in their twenties after they had moved to Los Angeles. At that time, Tina was divorced and a teacher, and Darlene was a TV writer/producer who had never married. Despite their differences, they shared common values and were extremely supportive of one another. Both say they have received more support for their growth from each other than from their own biological sisters.

Yet, as good as their relationship is, they have experienced major crises, one of the most serious being when Tina decided to quit teaching to "invade" Darlene's turf—TV writing. Initially, Darlene felt threatened by her friend's career switch. But soon the problems were smoothed out, and today Tina and Darlene remain tightly bonded, both successfully working in television.

When asked to compare her sisters-by-choice and her sisters-by-birth relationships, Tina responded that, for her, the "giving" parts of both relationships were the same. She was also close to—and concerned about—her younger sister, who had a history of emotional disturbance and frequent bouts with serious depression. It was helpful for her to have someone she could discuss her concerns for her sibling with and be able at the same time to give freely to both women.

"As close as I am to my sister by choice," Tina says, "some people still see it as merely a good friendship. After all, you don't have the same parents and the same complete background. But I just hope nobody ever asks me to save one of them if they are both drowning; I don't know what I'd do!"

Many women with biological sisters as well as sisters by choice have more faith in the biological bond. Tina says, "I have known Darlene since we were twelve years old, and through the years our friendship has grown and blossomed into a sisterly one. But when I think about it—and I can't believe I would say this because I trust her implicitly—I'm not one hundred percent sure that in a major crisis she would be there like my sister would. As erratic as my biological sister is, as crazy as she can be, I'd bet anything that if I was in major trouble, experiencing a crisis, she would be with me, no matter what. But even so, I am infinitely more comfortable and at ease with Darlene, and I'm hopeful she'd always be there for me."

Once women become aware of the distinctions between these two important relationships in their lives, they are often faced with the realization that their biological sisters—with whom they may not feel as close, with whom they do not share as many common interests, and from whom they may feel estranged—can still be the ones they would turn to in an emergency.

Once they are immersed in a sisters-by-choice relationship, some women express regret that they didn't appreciate their relationship with their biological sister. As Tina says, "I feel I took my sister for granted, and perhaps didn't treat her as well as I should have. But I think my friendship now with Darlene has enhanced the chances for improving my relationship with Cheryl, my natural sister, because I know what is possible with her now. I didn't even know that the chance for a substantial friendship existed before. In recent months, Cheryl and I have become closer since I've been able to develop a friendship with her apart from one based on and limited by our previous role assignments. In our case, she was the 'sick and crazy one' and I was the one whose feet were always firmly planted—you know, the 'dependable one.' "

Women like Tina and Cheryl—who, as youngsters, were separated by illness, age (in their case, seven years), or geographical distance—may never have the opportunity to explore the potential for friendship in their relationship. In their study of seventy-five volunteers between twenty and ninety-three years of age, Helgola Ross and Joel Milgram discovered that geographical distance and a wide age range between siblings often contribute to psychological distance.

In response to the need for a close tie, many of these women bond to their women friends, and it is then that, through their sister by choice, they may reconnect to their biological sisters.

As Karen Lindsey noted in *Friends as Family*, "The need for family—for nurturance, stability, sharing—does not stay behind when one leaves one's home." In fact, it is probably enhanced. Thus, women will very often make a strong familiallike commitment to their sisters-by-choice relationship.

Sisters by birth, sisters by choice—together, they define a woman's emotional life. Because of the tolerance a woman feels for her sister by choice, she may begin to view her natural sibling in a kinder light, becoming less demanding and less judgmental. And, in general, having a sister by choice affords a unique perspective on one's entire family.

We have seen that, even though sisters by choice do not share a family history, they do have a strong sense of loyalty, which is enhanced by the flexibility resulting from this lack of a biological connection. Sara, fifty-two, described her special camaraderie with her sister by choice, June, forty-eight: "We share many roles with each other—friend, mother, therapist, as well as sister. There's a pliability of roles I don't feel with my biological sister. With my natural sister, I am never asked for advice, and I don't feel valued as an individual who has grown, who has experiences to share, or who has something to offer. It seems there's a family script from a long time ago, and my part in the play is to be the one nobody listens to. It seems as if I have played that part for the last fifty-two years. June can say anything to me; if my sister said similar things, I would throw her out of my house. I feel June respects me, knows me, and understands my perspective better than anyone, including my husband. When she tells me something, even though I may not like it, I trust that she has my interests at heart."

But this wonderful feeling between female friends doesn't come for free. As you may recall, Tina had some doubts about how much she could depend on her chosen sister. In other instances, sisters by choice feel competitive toward one another. But, in general, because sisters by choice never had to compete for parental affection, their competition takes a different form and character and is usually limited to isolated incidents. One woman may yearn for the same recognition, love, and accomplishment that her friend experienced, but this is often soon replaced by a sincere enjoyment of her friend's good fortune. Unfortunately, because of the various historical factors and dynamics affecting a biological sisters relationship, a particular instance or event all too often becomes "loaded with meaning," and, as such, is not as easily resolved.

What of the family in all of this? When sisters by choice have been friends for many years, do they "adopt" each other's families? If one has a mother who has a tendency to pressure her, does the friend also feel pressure? How do they respond to these "other parents"?

Consider Joanne, at twenty-eight the oldest of three children, and Rhonda, twenty-seven, who has one younger sister, twenty-five. They were raised around the corner from each other in New York (where their families still live). Rhonda's mother had extremely high expectations for all of her children, and Joanne clearly recalls being considered one of her children: "From the time I was ten years old, I felt enormous pressure to achieve—not from my mother, but from Rhonda's mother! She was worse than my own mom. It was as if I had to take on an additional set of parents." To this day, Rhonda's mother conducts routine interrogations of her two "daughters."

Not long ago, Joanne and Rhonda bought a duplex in San Francisco. When asked about family rivalries, Rhonda, who has a somewhat rivalrous relationship with her younger sister, responded, "Joanne and I feel competitive within my family, not hers. For example, my father was out here visiting, and I had to go to a fund raiser, so Joanne and my dad went out to dinner. That dinner was six months ago and I still bring it up! *They had entirely too good a time!*" In some families, then, sisters by choice do compete for a parent's attention.

When two other sisters by choice, Dawn, thirty-three, and Evie, thirty-two, were recently visited by Evie's parents for the first time, Evie's mother, who had already heard so much about Dawn, invited Dawn to lunch while Evie was working. They immediately felt a special closeness, and she began to affectionately refer to Dawn as her "other daughter." This started to become problematic, however, when she began to ask Dawn personal questions about Evie's life. Dawn immediately redirected the inquiries, knowing that this "behind-the-back" communication would jeopardize her friendship with Evie.

Despite the problems parents can create in a sisters-by-choice relationship, however, biological sisters are the biggest troublemakers in friendships between women. Mitzi visited her sister, Rhonda, in San Francisco. Rhonda described it this way: "She lived with me for three months last year. I was glad to have her, but what really annoyed me was that she could have these long, intimate, soul-searching discussions with Joanne, but she and I would fight just like we always have."

Many feelings come into play when sisters by choice feel a part of their chosen sister's family, yet experience some uneasiness with their own natural siblings, and such feelings are heightened when the relationship between biological sisters is already strained, as with Rhonda and Mitzi. Also, when natural siblings are separated by geographical distance, and/or if one of them wants to become closer, she may feel jealous of the bond between her sister and her sister's dear friend. It is important to realize that some women are extremely possessive of their biological sisters and are bound to resent *any* woman who threatens their sibling bond. Indeed, the source of their jealousy may not actually be the other woman—far more compelling is their despair over their perceived inability to have a similarly close relationship.

This is quite a different sentiment than the one usually heard from teenagers who, in their eagerness to carve out their rightful place in their families, schools, or clubs, want desperately to have their *own* friends who are apart from the family and are not to be shared. "She's *my* friend!" a young girl will possessively remind her sister, implying, "You get your own!"

Interestingly, an examination of the character and the temperament matches of sisters by choice, as compared to those of biological sisters, shows that when women choose their friends, they tend to select those who bring out aspects of themselves that are quite different from those emphasized by their sisters. In other words, they seem to have qualitatively different relationships with their sisters by choice because the very nature and rationale for the relationship is different—unfettered by family roles, and fulfilling needs for both parties that are quite distinct from that of the biological bond. And why not? Being related by blood does not necessarily insure that this person is going to be everything you need and desire in a close female relationship. Very often the sisters-by-choice relationship offers the best of both worlds: the typically familial connections of loyalty, support, protection, and jealousy, *without* the complications intrinsic to the family dynamic.

The sisters-by-choice bond, then, is unique and need not necessarily be viewed by biological sisters as a threat. In fact, it can and should be perceived as something positive and enriching. No single person can fill all of your needs, and a sisters-by-choice friendship can act as a barometer for the "reality level" of your expectations for your biological sisters relationship. And your sibling may learn to appreciate that, when your needs are being met by a variety of sources, the demands upon her may be lessened. You may become more accepting of her, more understanding of her limitations, and therefore better able to appreciate her strengths.

While biological sisters relationships can and often are fulfilling, enriching, and forceful, they can thrive *alongside* a sisters-by-choice bond. Perhaps this helps explain why biological sisters who get along well with their siblings are rarely threatened by their sister's close friendships.

But every relationship goes through rocky times, and the strongest sisters-by-choice bond is not exempt. Jane, thirty-six, found herself in such a situation with her sister by choice, Rochelle, thirty-eight: "About two years ago, she went through a wide swing in her view of the world and her relationships with other people, and consequently has sort of turned off from me. I have tried to approach her, but she isn't interested. I've decided to just let her go through whatever she needs to go through. It appears that she is divorcing her husband, her job, and her best friend—me. I want her to know that I love her and I'll do whatever I can to help her, but she won't let me in. The interesting thing is that I don't know if I would have gotten through this without my two biological sisters. They have been wonderful. Each realizes what a confusing loss this is for me. They have understood who Rochelle is in my life through all of these years. She hasn't been seen as a threat to them. So they just want to help me get through this as easily as possible. They are such special people to understand that my love for her doesn't mean I love them any less; it's just a different kind of friendship.

"In talking about this over the past several months, my

sisters and I have become much more aware of the apparent fragility of some relationships. I am sure that my relationship with Rochelle is not over, but it is going through some sort of 'phase,' which makes me so clearly aware of who she is in my life. I cannot imagine a similar estrangement from my biological sisters. I will do anything to prevent it from happening."

For many women, a sister by choice can provide nurturing, freedom of expression, and acceptance of each other, under the most trying of circumstances. Lenore, forty-nine, and Judith, fifty-one, share a bond more intense and devoted than either woman has with her biological sister. Friends since grammar school, they live near each other and have served as "aunts" to each other's children. In addition to raising their own offspring, Lenore and her husband are responsible for the care of two foster girls, one of whom had been in Lenore's care for two years when her suspicions that the child had developmental difficulties were confirmed by her pediatrician. Unclear about what to do, she embarked on a multifaceted time-consuming, educational program, and subsequently decided to begin proceedings to legally adopt the child herself: "I wouldn't have had the courage and fortitude to go through all of these tests, clinical visits, and legal matters if it hadn't been for Judith. She came with me to our appointments, even though I hadn't asked her to. She just showed up the morning of the first appointment and asked if I'd like her to go. She said that if she were in my position, she would probably want me to be with her. Together, we tried to figure out what all of the doctors and specialists were talking about. Now we're enrolled in a parent program with mandatory attendance two days and one night a week, and she always comes with me. I didn't think our feelings for each other could grow after all these years, but they continue to climb to new heights. When I think of all the things I have to be grateful for in this world, I think of my family and of Judith, who is a part of me and my family."

When asked about *her* perception of their relationship, Judith said, "There's no way I can put into words the place we have in each other's lives. It's not either of our styles to tell the other what we mean to each other, and yet there is nothing—and I mean *nothing*—that we wouldn't do for each other or each other's families."

Sharon, a young Chicago woman, entered into a sisters-by-choice relationship without the slightest idea of what a close female friendship is like—partly because her relationship with her biological sister was characterized by hostile and competitive feelings. But in spite of the many obstacles she herself set up, the sisters-by-choice relationship flourished: "I thought all women would be like my sister and her friends, kind of bitchy, back-stabbing, and not to be trusted under any circumstances. Then I met Amanda through work, and we were assigned to a project together and needed to work long, hard hours, often into the evening. She would bring in homemade snacks and often would orchestrate our breaks around some classical music concert that was on the radio. She kept extending herself as a friend as well as a co-worker, and she didn't seem to want anything in return. This was all new to me. In my family, you never gave anything without expecting something in return. On the day of our presentation, she suggested we celebrate a job well done. That evening, I opened up to her a little bit. She was great; she disclosed some things about herself too, and the friendship just kind of evolved from there."

When asked what this friendship has meant to her, Sharon replied, "To me, it means sanity. Now, no matter what's happening in my life, I can discuss it with Amanda. We kind of check in with each other. We've known each other for twelve years now. Before meeting her, I used to think that you couldn't share anything personal or meaningful, that you couldn't be vulnerable because you would get it in the back!

"Today, my friendship and feeling for Amanda is more like that of a sister than what I have with my own sister. I haven't seen my real sister in fifteen years, and I really don't care if I ever see her again. I know that sounds harsh—maybe someday I will feel differently, but I doubt it. When my father was dying of cancer, the person I felt the closest to was Amanda. She always knew what to say to me and could tell by the look on my face when to leave me alone or when to ask if I wanted to talk. She just has a sense about me, and I for her. And I have to admit that it was Amanda who taught me how to trust. I never learned that in my family, and I fear that were it not for her I would have continued throughout my life never allowing anyone in."

Not all sisters-by-choice relationships are so serious and laden with meaning. Many women exhibit a more lighthearted side of themselves. Nina, forty-six, a university professor, told me that the only person with whom she can be totally "goofy" is Alice, forty, a bank president. Obviously, these two professionals need to maintain an impeccable image with their business associates—but when they are together, they can relax and be themselves. Alice says, "There's no one else in the world but Nina who would allow me to do what I do and not think I am totally 'whacko,' to say nothing of asking, 'How can this dame run a bank?' And can you imagine one of her students overhearing our conversations about our social lives, sex, our fears of getting older, and all the other things we discuss?"

Whether it is a close or a distant natural-sister relationship, or a sisters-by-choice relationship, all women can benefit from an intimate friendship such as Alice and Nina's. It is important for everyone to have someone with whom they can share their innermost selves. But the sisters-by-choice relationship invariably elicits ambivalent feelings from the women's families. There's a sense of both apprehension and relief at the presence of this person in their daughter's or sister's life—the "threat" stemming from the fact that this stranger may be privy to "family secrets"; the relief emanating from a genuine, altruistic desire for this person they love to have someone with whom she can share her innermost self.

Sometimes women wonder how their biological sisters can so openly share their lives with a "stranger." This is a manifestation of their resentment of this third party. When Geraldine, forty-one, and her biological sister, Maura, thirty-eight, had lunch with Deborah, Geraldine's sister by choice, Deborah asked how her son was getting along. Maura, unaware that Geraldine had shared the boy's drug-abuse problems with Deborah, nonchalantly told her everything was fine and, in kind, asked how Deborah's children were doing. Deborah responded, "It's okay, Maura, you can talk about it; I know."

Maura was shocked. She looked at Geraldine and said, "What is she talking about?" Geraldine responded that when she'd heard that Ben, Maura's son, had become involved with drugs, she had needed someone to talk to and had confided in her best friend. But, to Maura, Deborah was an outsider, and she wasn't comfortable with an outsider knowing so much about her life. She felt betrayed.

Later, in a phone conversation with Geraldine, Maura said, "How dare you tell her so much of my personal life? If she's your friend, you tell her about *your* life, not mine." Geraldine responded, "What happens to you and your son is part of my life. I needed to bounce my feelings off someone I could trust. She is our friend."

But Maura wasn't convinced. "She's not *my* friend, she's *your* friend, and I won't have you discussing my personal family business with her. I felt as if I was standing there naked. I know she meant well in asking, but it really is none of her business, and I don't want to air our dirty laundry in the neighborhood. If you have anything you want to discuss that has to do with my family, you discuss it with me."

Cecile, fifty-two, felt threatened by her fifty-year-old sister Agnes's friendship with Selma. Gradually, she stopped talking to Agnes about anything of importance, and though she would sometimes politely ask Agnes about Selma, she was so preoccupied with her feelings of insecurity about Selma's place in her sister's life that she couldn't really listen.

Problems like these should be confronted and resolved. Sisters by choice often want to be as many things to each other as possible, and very often do not have a hard time asking for what they want from one another. Birth sisters, on the other hand, may not even *know* exactly what it is they want from each other—and if they do, they have a hard time expressing it. This is exacerbated by jealousy of their sister's friends.

Ideally, sisters by birth and sisters by choice should get

along famously. Indeed, they often do. Recently three sets of sisters and their respective sisters by choice attended a sisters conference. Two of the sisters by choice had only male siblings and had always wanted sisters; one was an only child.

"I learned how to share and how to be a sibling from Lynn," Sandy, thirty-seven, and an only child, commented. "I never knew how much went on between siblings until I became so attached to Lynn and got a closer look at her two sisters."

At best, a sister by choice is a special friend who can enrich the life of not only her "selected sister," but also that woman's family members, *including* any biological siblings. At worst, a sisters-by-choice relationship can spark a variety of problems. And yet, regardless of the difficulties, most women treasure their sister by choice, and the obstacles seem like petty annoyances to be faced— and conquered.

CHAPTER 10

HOW PARENTS CAN ENCOURAGE THEIR DAUGHTERS TO FEEL CLOSE

"I wish my daughters the same kind of feelings that their aunts and I have for one another. We are as different as we are close!"

We have explored the options available to us for repairing and improving our damaged sibling bonds. But wouldn't it be wonderful if we could have *prevented* some of these problems from developing? That's where the parents as role models come into play. By instilling in a child a strong sense of self, a parent gives that child a better chance of having something meaningful to contribute to a sisters bond. But how do children develop such a sense of themselves?

We see ourselves as others see us. So analyzing this "looking-glass self" can be very helpful. For the majority of children, the treatment they receive from their parents is a major factor in how they perceive themselves, and all too often, parents inadvertently lead their offspring into relationships characterized by envy, hatred, and distrust, at the same time saying, "Love your sister; she's the only one you have." It's called giving double messages. The results? Ambivalence and confusion.

Since problems in sisters relationships usually begin in childhood, parents *can* take steps early on to strengthen the bond between their daughters. I'd like to offer suggestions now as to how parents can assist their children by providing an enriching, supportive, loving environment for them.

For example, children can be taught to be supportive and appreciative of each other's accomplishments, even when these achievements are in the same field. There is room in the family for two pianists or two tennis players. When a child is able to take pride in her own achievements, she will not feel the need to diminish her sister in order to feel secure within herself. In a sense, each child should be raised as an only child, regarded as a distinct and separate human being with unique talents.

Unfortunately, many parents were not involved in positive sibling relationships when they were children and see no alternative than to perpetuate the same parenting style they experienced. But this need not be the case. Patterns *can* be changed—but only if parents really want to.

I am convinced that most parents fully intend to do the best job of parenting that they possibly can—yet all too often circumstances interfere that inhibit the development and maintenance of a positive, loving family environment. For example, perhaps the parents simply don't know how to create the best possible home situation. Or maybe they themselves suffer from low self-esteem. In a now classical study of the self-esteem of ten-year-olds, Dr. S. Cooper-smith discovered that children with high self-esteem tended to have parents with high self-esteem, and, in general, the relationship between the generations was characterized by an ease in interacting and a genuine compatibility. With the responsibilities of the parents clearly defined, these children received encouragement and support. Through specific, everyday demonstrations of affection and concern and a generally close rapport, the parents communicated their acceptance of their children. By contrast, parents of insecure children usually had low self-esteem themselves and tended to deal more harshly with their youngsters. They did not establish and enforce guidelines for their children and had more difficulty expressing affection toward them.

But parents can learn to promote an accepting environment for each of their children. Two sisters, Elsa and Marta, were raised in a positive, healthy environment that emphasized individuality and cooperation. Even though their interests were in the same area—one of the sisters played the violin, the other the cello—Elsa and Marta were taught as children to accept and appreciate each other's talents. They are now both nationally known performers and teach at a major university in California, where they continue to be supportive of one another.

What ingredients exist in this family that are absent in other families? How can cooperation and appreciation be integrated into everyday family life? Well, it's not easy. First, the parents must *believe it* themselves. Then they might also establish a daily discussion period, during which each person in the family contributes what he or she feels is of value in his/her life.

Consider Abby, eight, who is presently trying to master

bicycle riding. Her family gives her accomplishments on the open road *as much attention* as her eleven-year-old sister Becky's efforts with Bach at the piano. In this family, the emphasis is not on which is more important in the world; rather, each child's skills and achievements—in her world at this time in her life—are not only acknowledged, but *rewarded.*

Sisters also need to learn that they can be relied on to help out in time of need. To this end, parents can set up situations in which sisters help each other. Feeling there is support from all family members also helps temper the threat of any perceptions of favoritism.

Children can also learn to value a sibling's opinion by seeing that their parents give credence to everyone's point of view. Of course, sophistication in problem solving is a skill that comes with age, but parents can get into the habit of presenting one sibling with a problem that the other is having. In discussing these dilemmas, children can be taught perspective and empathy—vital to a healthy sisters bond—and all too often found lacking. When children acquire these traits early in life, they tend to become so tightly incorporated into the child's behavioral repertoire that, gradually, they come naturally—and serve the adult sister very well indeed.

Not all families, of course, encourage this or any other kind of positive communication by or between children. Years ago, I ate dinner with a co-worker, her husband, and her two daughters, aged nine and seven. After taking our places at the table, Gretchen, the nine-year-old, tried several times to tell her father what had happened at school, but each time he quieted her, saying that when he wanted to hear from her, he would address her; until that time, she was to remain silent and sit like a lady. If she was good, after dinner he would give her five minutes to talk, before the TV news began.

I thought perhaps this was being done for my benefit, so I said, "Oh, don't worry about me, just go on as normal." The father glared at me and advised that this *was* normal. In his view, he added, girls had nothing to contribute to a dinnertime conversation. Gretchen sat back, politely listening to the adults' conversation, obviously eager—but unable—to contribute something. Her father told me that when she turned thirteen, she would be allowed to participate in the conversations at dinner. Until then, she should be seen and not heard. Just like it had been in his childhood.

Later during the meal, Gretchen and her sister, Christine, began playing with their food, giggling, and banging their feet against the chairs. Gretchen tried to make Christine laugh by sticking our her tongue while she was chewing. Gretchen's strategy worked, and *both* girls were sent off to bed—missing the opportunity to tell the family about their day.

These girls were being raised under an impossibly tyrannical reward system. This is not to say that the girls' dinner table antics were appropriate. They weren't—especially with company present. But perhaps if they hadn't felt so ignored by the adults, they wouldn't have resorted to these attention-getting devices.

The mother told me later that her husband had insisted that the girls be quiet throughout mealtimes. She knew they wanted to talk to him and gain his approval, but there were often weeks when they would have no interaction with him at all. She suspected that her daughters' creativity and sense of self-worth were suffering, but she felt forced to comply with her husband's demands, and she was at a loss as to what to do. When her husband was not there, she made every effort to appear interested in her daughter's activities, but in his presence she was afraid of undermining his stance on how children should be raised, so she, too, insisted that they be "ladies."

But when will Gretchen and Christine have an opportunity to be themselves? When will they be able to know that they are intrinsically okay, just as they are? Are these two girls going to grow up allied as a team against their father? Will they devalue each other's accomplishments, interests, and ideas because their own are devalued?

When a child feels that her accomplishments and thoughts are valuable, then she can more willingly offer a part of herself to her sisters, safe in the knowledge that her own position in the family is secure and treasured. This way, her sister's accomplishments are not perceived as threats, but even, in some cases, as inspirations. In these cases, sisters can (and usually do) enjoy their sister's achievements.

Allie, fifteen, proudly went to all of her sister's rehearsals for a school play, even though some of them cut into her own schedule. She wanted her sister, Brooke, thirteen, to know that the rehearsals were as important to her as the final performance, and that she appreciated Brooke's efforts.

This sibling support has been consistent from the start. When Brooke wanted to try out for the play, Allie helped her practice her lines by reading the other character's part. She was proud when Brooke landed the role and asked if she could attend one of the rehearsals. Brooke wavered— she didn't feel she was good enough yet. But Allie explained that she wanted to see Brooke grow into the role. She had thought about how she would feel in Brooke's position—practicing all the time for that day when all the people you love see you in the final performance—but she really was interested in the whole process. Brooke finally acquiesced, and Allie attended as many rehearsals as she could, listening carefully to Brooke's assessment after each one, offering her ideas *only when asked.* This experience marked the beginning of Allie's vital and supportive role in Brooke's budding acting career.

How had Allie developed this emotional maturity? Both girls had always been encouraged to appreciate each other *as individuals*—neither one better or worse, each one's differences making her *unique.* Because each was encouraged to pursue her own talents, to be the best that she could be (regardless of what her sister or anyone else was doing), they were able to grow as individuals and together. And they were able to get to know themselves *through* each other. Although not compared to each other, they were encouraged to observe and value each other's accomplishments and to recognize the lessons to be learned from "failures."

Comparing siblings probably has the most important effect on the sisters bond. Most of the women I talk to say emphatically, "Don't compare!" But, regardless of what the parents do, many children compare anyway—they can't help it. They look at their sister's accomplishments and failures and immediately assess where and how *they* measure up. It's perfectly natural. But when parents encourage this tendency by setting their children up for comparison, they are promoting a contest. And we all know that in every contest there's a winner and a loser. That's fine for gin rummy, but life with a sister should not be constant competition. Why can't they *both* be winners? Of course, healthy competition can and should be a part of their relationship—but it should be only *one* aspect, and it should *enhance* the relationship. Don't hear yourself say, "Your sister made honor roll, you have to too!" Or, "All of our daughters were presidents of the class; you must follow in the tradition." Or, "Your sister really made a mess out of her life; we need you to do us proud and prove that we didn't raise two losers."

Parents often hope their offspring can provide them with whatever they feel is lacking in *their* lives—and for this very reason they may be less inclined to encourage their children to become the best that they can be. They may require that their children perform certain functions within the family, at the expense of the youngsters' own interests and goals. An example is the mother who insists that her daughter be the "strong one," discouraging development of her sensitive, vulnerable side. As a result of this, the daughter may come to resent the sibling who has been "allowed" to explore her weaker side.

Sometimes, parents' needs inhibit daughters from developing strong connections and healthy respect for each other. One single mother, finding herself still depressed two years after her divorce, wanted her adult daughters to be available to her whenever she felt lonely. Needless to say, this interfered with their own social lives, and the young women actually found themselves engaged in a competition over which one was going to "babysit" their mother. When the older one wanted to go out, she would bribe the younger one to stay with their mother. In spite of this, the girls did gradually begin to feel closer to each other. Unfortunately, they became increasingly distant from their mother and resentful of her apparent inability to "get herself together."

To make matters worse, when the mother was in the

company of either of her daughters (it didn't seem to matter which one), she would discuss how close she felt to her, implying that the other one didn't give her the same kind of comfort. After comparing notes the sisters confronted their mother, saying they were tired of her efforts to pit one against the other, and insisting they each be allowed to comfort her in their own way.

Most parents find that from time to time they actually do have favorites among their children. As psychologists Stephen Bank and Michael Kahn point out in *The Sibling Bond*, "Favoritism occurs in all families. But in well-functioning families, children are favored for different characteristics. Or they are favored on different days, or at different periods of their lives, so that on the whole no child clearly prevails."

Parents should not send an insincere message to those children who, for whatever reason, are not in the spotlight at a given moment—it can only widen the rift between them. Parents should instead assure a child constantly of their love, trying to find and then focusing on whatever aspects of the child's behavior or personality they can appreciate. Parental attention should be balanced so that there is no clear "favorite" for long. Some parents say that because they love all of their children equally, they will have to treat them all equally; but it is hard to do this, and although this is certainly an admirable goal, Dr. Robert Bolton notes that parents too often end up relating on the basis of the lowest common emotional denominator.

If a father, for instance, does find that his preference for one child persists and is reflected in his behavior, then it's time to do something about it. He should find out if the other child's behavior is reminiscent of aspects of himself that he doesn't like. Does the child remind him of an ex-spouse? Why is there such tension? The parent must make a concerted effort to change the way he interacts with the child, and even with the rest of the family. For a child's healthy development, it is absolutely critical that she feel she is loved by her parents and that she is a person of value.

There are many other issues associated with the raising of daughters. Whenever I'm asked, "Should sisters be dressed alike?" I know that no matter how I respond the sisters will continue to be dressed identically because "it's cute," and there's something about "matching siblings" that goes over well at those family picnics. Ultimately, however, the older sister starts balking, usually about one or two years before her mother or father relents and lets them out of the house in clothes that suit each of them *as individuals*.

Clothes are a potentially volatile issue between adolescent siblings, one that is emblematic of deeper needs and problems. "Get out of my closet" is a cry heard frequently in homes with two or more sisters. What's behind this family struggle over clothing? Often, a sister decides that her sweater makes a definitive statement to her family and, indeed, to the world about who she is. She decides that in essence it *is* her identity at this stage in her life, and therefore she isn't likely to be sympathetic when a younger sister wears the sweater to see what adolescence is like through the eyes of an actual teenager's clothes.

In cases like this, parents can play a major role in protecting the rights of each of their children. Some parents insist upon the "share and share alike" philosophy—and yet this is insensitive to a daughter's natural need to have something of her very own. There are also families who advocate keeping all possessions separate—locked away in closets and drawers; others like the idea of "community cupboards." No matter what system is implemented, it should be applied consistently and equitably to *all* siblings.

To this end, it's not enough to establish rules; just as bedtime rules must be adjusted as children grow older, so must guidelines for sharing respond to the changing needs of *each* child.

One woman at a sisters seminar in San Francisco told of her family's "community closet" for her five sisters. *All* of the girls' clothes were kept in that closet and were to be shared, with the exception of two items put aside for each girl. No one was allowed to take those items without her permission. Community closts can work well *only* if the girls treat their clothes in a similar manner.

Separate closets work well for some families, although quite often girls discover that their best shirt has either disappeared or is lying at the bottom of the closet rolled up into a ball. In such cases, parents should intervene, but only to remind their daughters of the rules—*not* to judge or take sides. The role of a parent is, again, to serve the siblings equally, without showing preference. "You always take her side, she can do no wrong" is an often-heard complaint when a parent intervenes.

Even if a problem does *seem* to get solved by parental intervention, this way of dealing with family conflicts does not always teach sisters to get along better in the world. Having siblings affords a child the opportunity to learn about sharing, solving problems, and asserting her rights—without manipulating or dominating the other person. Ideally, having a sibling can help a youngster learn the rules of the games she will be playing for the rest of her life. In this regard, parents can *assist* their children in working out problems, while allowing them to develop skills of their own as well. If a child seems interested only in "slugging it out," parents need to offer alternative ways of dealing with her anger. But instead of saying, "Don't be mad at your sister; you love her," parents should give her words that match her feelings, along with actions that are assertive and appropriate and will not dominate or manipulate her sister. In *Between Parent and Child* and *Between Parent and Teenager,* psychologist Haim Ginott suggests that parents accept their children's feelings with sympathy and understanding so that their children know their parents are with them—not against them. A parent can say, "You feel mad and I'll bet you don't like talking to her at all!"

Sibling conflict takes many forms. Older, more strictly raised daughters may complain, "How come when I was her age, I couldn't go out? Now you let her get away with murder! Why did I have to be the 'groundbreaker' for the family?"

But if an older daughter feels appreciated by her siblings for her efforts, she is more likely to be accepting of changes in family rules. Psychologist Robert Sears and his associates noted years ago that later-born children tend to be treated with more spontaneity and unconditional acceptance than earlier-born offspring. And if younger siblings are given certain privileges not offered to older ones at the same age, the older children may end up resenting everyone in the family. To prevent such sibling resentment from snowballing, it is essential to discuss any new rules openly. This way, sisters can become allies instead of adversaries.

Lavonne, sixteen, and Marie, fifteen, were trying to convince their parents to change the "dating-age rule" so that Marie would be able to attend her school dance. Convinced that the rule was unfair and that Marie was mature enough to go, Lavonne "lobbied" on behalf of her younger sister, even though *she* had had to wait until she was sixteen to accept her first date. The entire family discussed the reasons for the rule, and the parents agreed to lower the age limit.

If parents fail to help their children explore alternative ways of handling conflict, the children may never learn them. Although parents are primarily providers of love, it is also up to them to protect and teach the problem-solving skills that will help their children become independent, confident, and able.

Unfortunately, not all parents have adequate teaching skills or are able to communicate openly with their children. As discussed in Chapter 8, parents should indeed assess what kind of feeling they are transmitting. Is it nonpossessive love? Is it a genuine attempt to empathize with their children and with each other? Carl Rogers, Milton Mayerhoff, and others have noted that these qualities are essential for improving communication. Yet it is difficult for a parent to teach them to their children if they are not incorporated into their lives as adults and, more important, as parents.

Siblings who know that they are unconditionally loved *can* develop loving feelings toward each other; they may not necessarily always like what the other does, but at least they will be receptive in a nonjudgmental, uncritical fashion. This is not to suggest that parents should never criticize their children—just that they must be careful about *how* they do it. If they decimate the child's self-esteem in the process, what good has it been?

Still another relevant issue—raised earlier in this book—

is that of labels. Parents must recognize the ramifications of descriptive labels assigned to children early on. If some of these names—and they're often pejorative—stick, they may be internalized by the child and carried well into adulthood. A more positive approach is for parents to use labels to suit a particular situation, and overall to see their youngsters as constantly evolving, *growing* individuals.

Siblings can also be encouraged to relate to each other more positively by *asking* each other for help, instead of *demanding* it. When a child orders her sibling to do something for her, the typical response is "Why should I?" That leads to such reactions as "Because I said so, and I'm older—so you have to listen to me!" However, siblings can be taught by their parents to offer reasons that children can understand. (They don't have to like them, but they can understand them.)

Theresa, thirteen, and Gloria, nine, were told to wait after the movies at 5:30 for their mother to pick them up. But the film ended earlier than expected, and Gloria suggested that the two of them buy an ice cream in a store two blocks from the theater. Theresa thought it would be safer if they stayed in front of the theater, where it was well lit and crowded. Gloria was upset, but she accepted the explanation much more readily than if Theresa had simply said no. True, it took Theresa a little longer to respond this way—maybe thirty or forty seconds longer—but the exchange was much more specific and meaningful for *both* girls.

There are ways for parents to create an environment that promotes open, supportive communication. First, parents should carefully avoid asking questions that do not require much of a response. If siblings get the message that a simple yes or no is enough, they may decide to keep *all* of their news to themselves—and they may very well carry this style into adulthood. I don't suggest that parents delve into a child's privacy (depending on her age, privacy can be an extremely important issue), but I do advise that parents be sensitive to the quality of their communication with their children.

As for sisters themselves, how can they learn to respect and accept one another if they don't know how the other feels, what she does, what she values? Indeed, if each begins to *assume* that her sister is functioning and viewing the world in a manner similar to her own, the ensuing breakdown in communication can have severe ramifications for the sisters bond.

If sisters are to respect and know each other, they must air their differences. If they are encouraged to talk to each other *and* to their parents, they can learn the skills—from a very early age—that are essential in asserting their own needs, *without* infringing on their sister's rights. At the same time, they will still learn to listen to their sister and respond with interest and empathy. Without this kind of openness, they may never learn to express their feelings and/or listen to each other's responses with concern and compassion.

Unfortunately, most of us have not been taught to be good listeners, and we very often find it difficult to learn these skills in adulthood. As a parent, however, you can serve as a good model, demonstrating your interest in what your child has to say by looking at her when she talks, by sitting down with her and offering five or more minutes of your undivided attention—*never* giving the impression that you would rather be elsewhere. This tells the child that what she says is important.

In addition, if one child is talking to you and a sibling or other family member tries to get your attention, the first child needs to know that she will not be interrupted. The other person's "special time" with you will be respected as well, but for the moment remind the others that their sister was not yet finished relating a story, or hadn't yet come to the point. You'll be an excellent role model for a polite and effective way to avoid interruptions.

Jenny, twelve, is very articulate and loves to talk to her mother when she gets home from school. Her sister, Sandra, eleven, doesn't speak as fast as Jenny, and whenever she begins to talk, Jenny is all over her to "Hurry up, I don't have all day." Their mother has to remind both girls that Sandra can take as long as she needs to get her thoughts together.

One afternoon I heard the girls discussing the rock video of singer Michael Jackson's *Thriller* album, which they both had seen the night before. Sandra was petrified when the graves opened and the corpses started dancing around the streets with Michael Jackson. In her typically slow fashion, she described the scene in detail. All the while, Jenny kept reminding her sister that she, too, had seen the videotape and there was therefore no need to go through it line by line. Her own comments were related to how great she thought *Thriller* was, how realistic and disgusting the corpses were, and how silly her sister was to be such a "baby."

As they spoke, Sandra began feeling worse and worse. Fortunately, their mother finally stepped in and asked why they both couldn't have been right. Wasn't it true that *Thriller* was a frightening tape if you were a person who was inclined to get scared by thoughts of ghosts, ghouls, and bizarre images? And yet, if you weren't one to become terrified by those things, couldn't it be thought of as funny? Without making either of the girls feel uncomfortable, their mother highlighted the differences between them and encouraged each girl to see her perspective in a positive light.

There is no "right" way to parent sisters. There are, however, ways to create an environment in which children can feel valued and comfortable with themselves and have a positive view of their own worthiness and their roles as siblings. Interactions between parents and daughters should be characterized by unbiased, unconditional love. Under such circumstances, a sisters bond will flourish.

Now is the time to take a long, hard look at your relationship with your sister. It may take work, there may be times when you wonder if it's worth all the trouble—even pain—but let me assure you that it is. Because what we're really talking about here is *getting close*, and that is one of life's richest rewards.

BIBLIOGRAPHY

Ackerman, Nathan. *Treating the Troubled Family*. New York: Basic Books, 1966.

Aldous, Joan. *Family Careers: Developmental Change in Families*. New York: John Wiley, 1978.

Arnstein, Helene S. *Brothers and Sisters: Sisters and Brothers*. New York: E. P. Dutton, 1979.

Atkins, Dale. "A Comparison of Older Sisters of Hearing-Impaired and Normally Hearing Children on Measures of Responsibility and Parental Attention." Ph.D. diss., University of California at Los Angeles, 1982.

Bank, Stephen and Michael Kahn. *The Sibling Bond*. New York: Basic Books, 1982.

Bertherat, Therese and Carol Bernstein. *The Body Has Its Reasons*. New York: Avon Books, 1976.

Bloomfield, Harold (with Leonard Felder). *Making Peace With Your Parents*. New York: Random House, 1983.

Ginott, Haim. *Between Parent & Child*. New York: Avon Books, 1965.

———. *Between Parent & Teenager*. New York: Macmillan, 1969.

Killmann, Ralph and Kenneth Thomas. "Interpersonal Conflict-Handling Behavior as Reflections of Jungian Personality Dimensions." *Psychological Reports* (37), 1975.

Koch, H. "Attitudes of Young Children Toward Their Peers as Related to Certain Characteristics of their Siblings." *Psychological Monographs,* 70 (19), 1956.

Laing, Ronald, H. Phillipson and A. Lee. *Interpersonal Perception: A Theory and a Method of Research.* New York: Springer Press, 1966.

Lamb, Michael. "Interactions Between Eighteen-Month Olds and their Preschool-Aged Siblings." *Child Development.* 48 (1), 1978.

Lamb, Michael and Brian Sutton Smith (eds.). *Sibling Relationships: Their Nature and Significance Across the Lifespan.* Hillsdale, N.J.: Lawrence Erlbaum Associates, 1982.

Lindsey, Karen. *Friends as Family.* Boston: Beacon Press, 1981.

Lederer, William and Don Jackson. *The Mirages of Marriage.* New York: W. W. Norton, 1968.

Mehrabian, Albert. "Communication Without Words." *Psychology Today.* September 1968.

Moustakas, Clark. *Individuality and Encounter.* Cambridge, Mass.: Howard A. Doyle, 1971.

Rogers, Carl. *Client-Centered Therapy: Its Current Practice, Implications and Theory.* Boston: Houghton Mifflin, 1951.

————. *On Becoming A Person.* Boston: Houghton Mifflin, 1961.

Sutton-Smith, Brian and Benjamin Rosenberg. *The Sibling.* New York: Holt, Rinehart & Winston, 1970.

Toman, Walter. *Family Constellation.* New York: Springer Press, 1969.

Watzlawick, Paul, Janet Beavin and Don Jackson. *Pragmatics of Human Communication.* New York: W. W. Norton, 1967.

Weisner, Thomas and R. Gallimore. "My Brother's Keeper: Child and Sibling Caretaking." *Current Anthropology,* 18, 1977.